IZZARD INK
PUBLISHING

INFLUENTIAL IMPACT

The Art of Significant Leadership

How to Grow People into Passionate Partners

By Dan Clark, CSP, CPAE
New York Times Best Selling Author
Hall of Fame Speaker

INFLUENTIAL IMPACT

The Art of Significant Leadership

How to Grow People into Passionate Partners

By Dan Clark, CSP, CPAE

ACKNOWLEDGEMENTS

To my dad S. Wayne Clark and mom Ruby Maughan Clark, who were the first leaders I can remember, who knew to teach me correct principles and let me govern myself.

To retired Air Force Generals John Jumper, Robert Oaks, Hal and Cynthia Hornburg, Mark and Betty Welsh, Bruce and Vickie Carlson, Frank Gorenc, Robin Rand, and Maryanne Miller, Lt. General Maggie Woodward, Lt. General Ken and Cindy Wilsbach, Maj. Generals Don Alston and most significantly Johnny Weida; and Army General Mike Scaparrotti, who have taught me through example and friendship the difference between commanding and controlling, and the significance of leading under pressure using the 'soft power' of influence, respect and admiration through example, instead of 'hard power' authority and title. I honor these amazing human beings who are true military heroes and friends driven by love, duty, sacrifice, service before self and commitment to excellence in all they do!

To my friends and mentors Dr. Normand Gibbons, Doug Miller, Fred Ball, Steve Cosgrove, Hal Bourne, Bob Mendenhall, Bill Gibbs, Bill Kimball, Bob Raybould, Homer Warner, Bob Whitman, Royden and Ali Derrick, Gary Mangum, Arnie Ferrin, Rick Warner, Steve Munn, Todd Peterson (Pete), Blain Hope, Clay Stringham, Brent Watts, Brent Bowen, Walter Plumb, Scott Keller, Randy Garn, David Ayre, Jason Bourne, David Spafford, Todd Larsen, Todd Cook, Mike Swenson, Todd Morgan, Brad Morris, Don (Doc) and MorMor Sansom, Sam Clark, Debbie Clark and Paul Clark, for illuminating for me the Art of Partner Leadership

To Danny, Nikola, McCall, and Alexandrea for finding wisdom, comfort, laughter, learning and solace in my speeches, stories, anecdotes, systems and words. I love you and need each of you in my life forever. And to My Sweet KC who is the leader of the Clark Clan and responsible for how well our kids turned out as leaders in their own homes, jobs, churches, neighborhoods, and world!

TABLE OF CONTENTS

INTRODUCTION

A man had a dream in which a genie came to him and explained that because he had lived a noble life, he would grant him one wish. The man thought for a minute and said, "I wish for happiness and success to fill the whole earth." The genie smiled and replied, "That's an honorable wish sir, but we don't deal in fruits here, we only deal in seeds."

As I travel the world it seems that everybody's wish is to be happy. The tragedy is that most never get it because they think it's found at a destination that's impressive. No. Happiness is the residual benefit and positive effect that can only come through doing something that produced it. Happiness is a positive "fruit" that we harvest because of specific seeds we have sown.

The same holds true for achieving success. Success is defined as "producing any result." However, because losing and failing are results, what we need to seek is the level beyond success I call "significance," where we don't just get what we think we want at the moment. We seek to achieve a "desired result" so we want what we get. Becoming a "Significant Leader" begins when we determine which "fruit" we desire and with an understanding of the Law of the Harvest (We Reap Only What We Sow) we focus on planting the specific seed that will produce our desired fruit. It's more than cliché' to say input equals output 100 percent of the time.

This begs the question: does your desired result only require that you plant a seed that will yield only an impressive short-term success, or is it a seed that will bring forth important long-term significance?

When it comes to leadership, most leaders – at least the ones who have titles, believe the purpose of a leader is to expand the size of their 'tribe' and generate more 'Likes' on Facebook, and 'Views' on the internet/YouTube, so they only plant seeds to increase the number of their followers. This is wrong!

The purpose of a leader is to grow more leaders by planting the seeds of significance where you teach correct principles and laws, set specific mutually agreed upon expectations, and inspire others as your teammates and family members to govern themselves for the same reasons you do!

When this occurs, you realize the majestic difference between being a leader and being a 'Significant Leader' who now knows that the goal is not to gain a title that gives you permission to step up and lead. The goal is not to seek power and authority so you can tell people what to do. The goal is to learn to lead with influence, which requires no title, so people choose to follow you – not because they have to, but because they want to!

Significant Leaders know that standing in the front of the room and calling yourself a leader, no more makes you a leader than sitting in the middle of a garage makes you a truck! Leadership implies action! And when you initiate this type of inclusive invitational action you prove true that 'the things we help create we support,' which in turn transforms everybody in your organization into a 'Partner Leader' who now takes ownership of customer service with a desire to increase his/her personal productivity based on personal accountability.

Don't we love it when we go into a grocery store and don't have to find the manager to ask him/her where a certain something is? We can literally ask anybody who works there in any department, and they willingly walk us right to the isle and help us get our obscure item from the shelf.

Because we all want to interact with decision makers, the purpose of a leader is to turn everybody inside the organization into a creative thinker, decision maker and problem solving 'Partner.'

For this reason, I have written this book to remind you of why you should be this kind of Significant Leader, AND to give you the tactical tools and time-tested techniques to develop your people into a culture of 'Partner Leaders' within and without your organization.

Guaranteed, 'Partner Leadership' is the new leadership model that masterfully brings Millennials, GenExers and Baby Boomers together to form a deeply connected trusting team, executing as one heartbeat with a 'Growth Mindset' focused on creating an extraordinary customer experience for everybody involved in your enterprise. Cheers!

CHAPTER ONE

ROCK BOTTOM BELIEF

"Your life is the creation of your mind. When you become the master of your mind, you are master of everything. It can enslave you or empower you. It can plunge you into the depths of misery or take you to the heights of ecstasy. When you realize how powerful your thoughts are, you will never think a negative thought. Whatever you plant in your subconscious mind and nourish with repetition and emotion will one day become a reality. When you fill your mind with truth and positive thoughts, your life will start to change."

How many times in our lives, when everything seems to have gone wrong, have we described our sad and depressing situation by claiming, "I hit rock bottom." No. We did not hit rock bottom! We hit "Rock Foundation." We hit "Rock Belief System." We hit our baseline "Core Values" and bottom line 'Governing Principles" on which we were raised. We hit the place where we are forced to show our "true colors" grounded in the reality that "crisis does not make or break the man or woman – it just reveals the true character within."

In the corporate world, when the economy plummets and things start to unravel, the company does not hit rock bottom. It hits the foundational beliefs and cultural expectations on which the organization was founded and built.

It's no surprise that the reason 85% of family owned businesses fail by the third generation is because this 'grand child generation' is so far removed from the foundational beliefs of sacrifice and hard work that it took to start and build the business, that they feel 'entitled' and don't think they have to subscribe to the same core values that grandpa and grandma followed to keep it going.

So the question is: What do you believe – really? And are your beliefs deep enough and solid enough to keep you resilient and strong?

REAL LIFE SUPER HEROES

In my experience, there is not a man or woman on the planet who has greater mental toughness and a clearer comprehension of what he/she believes and why they believe it, than the United States Army Special Forces, Air Force Combat Controllers and Navy Seals. On one of my many military tribute tours 'down range' to speak to our combat troops in Iraq, Afghanistan, Africa and Asia, a Navy Seal taught me that "An armored up warrior never has to get ready – he/she stays ready!" – and "It's not enough to say, 'I will do my best.' We must succeed in doing that which is necessary!"

Whoa! Not a lot of wiggle room for whining, blaming, complaining or quitting! Which begs the questions: Were these fierce fighters born this way, or are they made? Are leaders born or made? More specifically, what do these extraordinarily strong, brave, courageous, resilient, focused super heroes believe that has allowed them to create this elite culture of integrity, unwavering trust, mutual respect, service before self and commitment to excellence in all they do?

In my observation every leader is made, and in the 'Profession of Arms,' every man and woman becomes a leader based on the foundational understanding that "Under pressure, you don't step up your game. You succumb to the level of your preparation, training and practice – which means pressure is not something that is naturally there. It's created when you question your own ability. When you know what you've been trained to do, there is never any pressure! That's why you train and practice so hard!"

Isn't this why we have company meetings and sales rallies and enroll in leadership training? The troubling thing to me is that most leadership gurus want us to begin with the end in mind and answer:

Where do you want to go? But the truth is: the only place from which people can grow and develop is where we are.

WHERE ARE YOU – RIGHT NOW – TODAY?

Everyday we need to start our day by asking: 'Where am I right now - in this moment: physically, intellectually, spiritually, emotionally, socially, financially, and with my family?' No matter where you go, there you are. A geographic relocation doesn't change much! You must stand up from where you sit and grow healthy and strong from where you are planted.

Whenever we book an UBER ride, we are required to enter in our present location. If we lie about where we are, the directions won't work! Getting clear and honest about your current reality is critical, because it's the time and space between reality and your vision of the future where all your personal and leadership development work is done! Your future depends on what you do in the present.

As I travel the world, having spoken to millions of people in over 68 countries, I continuously hear the leaders stating that Millennials are this, and GenExers are that, and Baby Boomers are neither this nor that - which means the conversation is always about what divides us and makes us different. For this reason alone, my presentations focus on the time-tested truths, tactical techniques and proven processes that have always worked and have never changed - regardless of the generation!

THE ANSWERS ARE STILL IN THE BOX!

This means that the next time someone tells you to 'think outside the lines' and look outside the box,' will you please join me in asking, 'What if the answers are still IN the box?' Most people who come to meetings and trainings and read books like this, do so in search of the new answers - when in reality, don't you think we should be searching for the right answers? And the right answers have always been right - in every generation - or we can't call them right!

For example, it doesn't mater if you are a Millennial, GenExer or Baby Boomer, the forever truth is that the purpose of a leader is to grow more leaders, who believe what you believe – not generate more followers. When we share a common belief we create 'Partner Leaders' who increase productivity based on their own personal accountability, realizing that the things we help create, we support.

When we help create an organizational culture that acknowledges there is a change happening in the world, where people want to live a meaningful life that actually matters, and feel genuinely wanted and valued within our companies, and emotionally engaged with our customers, suddenly **every Millennial, GenExer and Baby Boomer in the organization becomes a 'Partner Leader'** focused on something larger than them selves and obligated to exceed expectations – not because it is expected by leadership, but because it is demanded of them selves!

This means that everything required to take yourself and your organization to the next level is already inside of you. Every action you take is based on the strength or weakness of your foundational beliefs. Which takes us full circle back to what do you believe – really? What are the foundational core values that guide your personal decisions and inspire your organizational performance to break sales records and achieve the level beyond success?

CORE VALUES

Core values are the guiding principles that dictate behavior and action in an individual and an organization. They invite us to stay in tune with our conscience so we know what is right and wrong. They help our organizations determine if we are on the right path toward accomplishing our business goals. They influence the decisions we make every day.

The core values you choose help shape your identity. Core values are the rules and boundaries that define your company's culture and personality. In order for the people on your team to work together productively and efficiently, everyone needs to be on the same page.

Core values help provide the framework for determining whether you are on the right track so that you can course correct if necessary.

In one scenario, when everybody in an organization obligates them selves to the same rock solid, clearly understood, foundational truths, no matter what happens on the outside, they continue to thrive from the inside out. US Army General Douglas MacArthur said, "When we sweat more in peace we will bleed less in war."

However, when an organizational culture has a weak and ambiguous philosophical foundation that does not require total buy-in from everybody at every pay grade, 'a house divided against itself cannot stand.'

CHAPTER TWO

THE REAL POWER OF THE MIND

*"Whatever the mind can conceive and believe,
the mind can achieve."* – *Napoleon Hill*

So... what do you believe? And, are your beliefs big enough, deep enough, strong enough, true enough? How committed are you and your teammates to these beliefs and do you fully comprehend the power they possess?

ANDREW CARNEGIE

In my personal search to answer these questions it became obvious that the foremost authority on the power of our thoughts and beliefs is Napoleon Hill. Hill was commissioned by one of the world's most successful and wealthiest men, Andrew Carnegie, to create a book that would capture the secrets of mega success and enduring happiness. The book is called, Think and Grow Rich, which to this day continues to change the world. Read it!

As the story goes, when Carnegie asked Hill to embark on this assignment, Hill confessed that he was not fit for the job of creating this practical application of success principles because he was broke. That is when Carnegie replied, "All success begins with definiteness of purpose, with a clear picture in your mind of precisely what you want from life."

That left a great impact on Hill. But it was what Carnegie said next that completely altered the shape of his thinking forever, and allowed him to impact millions upon millions of people with his work:

"Everyone comes to the earth blessed with the privilege of controlling his mind power and directing it to whatever ends he may choose. Think of it as arriving with the equivalent of two sealed envelopes, one of which is labeled, 'the riches you may enjoy if you take possession of your own mind and direct it to ends of your own choice.' And the other is labeled, 'the penalties you must pay if you neglect to take possession of your mind and direct it.

In the one labeled 'riches' is this list of blessings: 1) sound health, 2) peace of mind, 3) a labor of love of your own choice, 4) freedom from fear and worry, 5) a positive mental attitude, 6) material riches of your own choice and quantity.

In the envelope labeled 'penalties' is this list of the prices one must pay for neglecting to take possession of his own mind: 1) Ill health, 2) fear and worry, 3) indecision and doubt, 4) frustration and discouragement throughout life, 5) poverty and want, 6) and evils consisting of endless greed, jealousy, anger, hatred and superstition.

Which envelope will you open, which literally will change the direction and outcome of the remainder of your life?"

WHAT DO YOU REALLY BELIEVE – REALLY?

There is pure power in our thoughts. What we think, we most certainly become. But why is that? How is that the mere concept of something, held in the forefront of our minds, can be brought to fruition through persistent application over time? While very little is known about our brains, and subsequently our minds, one thing is very certain. Whatever the mind can conceive and believe, it can achieve, no matter what the present circumstances or obstacles surrounding a situation.

Yet, many of us don't believe in this. We focus on what's wrong and what's bad and we ultimately steer towards that. We don't think that we can achieve anything that we conceive or believe in. In fact, it's quite the opposite. Our negative thinking turns into dark, fear-based thoughts filled with ominous what-if scenarios. It's easy to allow negative thinking to consume and frighten you into a state of inaction.

And when things are going bad, it seems to compound upon it self. We begin attracting negative situations, people and things into our lives.

But what happens when you do the opposite? What happens when you train your brain to think conversely and think only positive thoughts, focus only on positive purposes, and emulate only positive, productive, powerful people?

When it comes to our ability to turn each stumbling block into a stepping-stone and every set back into a comeback, it definitely will be easier to rise each time we fall when we deeply believe specific truths that equip us mentally and emotionally to adapt to change, overcome obstacles and be resilient.

TWELVE FOUNDATIONAL RESILIENCY TRUTHS

- The gem cannot be polished without friction, nor man perfected without trials.

- Adversity introduces us to our authentic selves and either makes us bitter or better.

- We shouldn't be so quick to claim our limitations when perhaps we've never truly tested them. We will never know how strong we are until being strong is our only choice.

- The greatest mistake we can make in life is to continually fear we will make one. If we are not failing a few times it means we're not pushing ourselves hard enough.

- Pain is a signal to grow not to suffer, which means in life there are no mistakes, only lessons – so we never really fail or lose because we always learn.

- Healing doesn't mean the damage never existed. It means the damage no longer controls our lives.

- What you've been in the past does not make you who you are today as much as what you plan to become in the future makes you who you are today.

- A broken clock is right twice a day. Never give up on anybody – especially yourself!

- You are under no obligation to be the same person you were a year, month, day, or even 15 minutes ago. You have the right to grow, and the only person you need to be better than is the person you were yesterday. However, you can only grow when you comprehend that sadness gives depth - happiness gives height. Sadness gives roots - Happiness gives branches. Happiness is like a tree going up into the sky, and sadness is like the roots going down into the womb of the earth. Both are needed. The higher a tree grows, the deeper it goes. The bigger the tree, the bigger the roots - simultaneous and in proportion.

- Dependence on another is perpetual disappointment.

- Character is developed in the workshop of our daily lives, practiced in the uneventful, commonplace routine of life, so in the great moments of test and trial, our character can be displayed.

- When you focus on your goals your fears go away. When you focus on your fears your goals go away. Change your focus – change your life!

YOU CAN ONLY IF YOU THINK YOU CAN

It is more than cliché to say "achieving greatness is mind over matter" – "will over skill," and that "no pain, no gain" really means "no heart, no chance!" Proof is found in the legendary tale of Olympic champion Shun Fujimoto.

Going into the 1976 Olympic Summer Games in Montreal, Canada, the Japanese Men's Gymnastics team had dominated the world, winning four consecutive Team Gold Medals in the previous four Olympics. However, it was gymnast Shun Fujimoto who, during these 1976 Games, helped his country win the Gold by hiding the fact that he had broken his leg earlier in the competition and continued with two further events.

Fujimoto knew that in such a tight contest with their closest rivals the Soviet Union, any dropped points would mean an end to that reign and huge disappointment for his country and his teammates. There was no way the Japanese team could win the Gold Medal if Fujimoto did not compete. What would you have done?

After sustaining his excruciating injury during his floor exercise, Shun moved to the next event and continued with his pommel horse routine, scoring 9.5 out of 10. When he dismounted he fought through the debilitating pain and moved on to the final event, the rings, without even a limp. Of course, he knew that even if he could make it through that last performance he would have to land on his injured leg and stand tall and steady-straight for three full seconds after a complicated spinning dismount from a height of almost three meters. And to add fuel to this fire, while Fujimoto waited the few minutes to compete, he and his coach calculated that he had to achieve a score of at least 9.5 in order for his team to win!

With every eye in the stadium glued on Fujimoto, and with his heart pounding and his leg throbbing, not only did Shun complete the routine, but he delivered the very best performance of his entire career, made a solid landing on both feet and remained standing, to record an incredible 9.7, despite dislocating his kneecap and tearing the ligaments in his broken leg in the process.

Doctors who watched and examined him afterwards remarked, “How he managed to do somersaults and twists and land without collapsing in screams is beyond my comprehension.”

In the film footage of his Olympic competition (which I have watched many times), as Fujimoto lands his routine, not only can you see what happens to his leg, but you can witness the grit, determination and personal courage in Shun’s face not to let the pain show.

Because of his heroic performance and dedication to sacrifice and commitment to service before self, Japan’s gymnastics team was able to defeat the Soviet Union team by four tenths of a point to win the Gold Medal for the fifth straight Olympic Games in a row!

CHAPTER THREE

ARE YOU SUCCESSFUL OR SIGNIFICANT?

"There is more hunger for love and human connection in this world than for food and money; more hunger for respect and appreciation than for position and power; more hunger for purpose and meaning than for fame and glory."

One of my American football teammates was drafted into the National Football League in the second round, which meant he received a huge signing bonus and a lucrative million-dollar contract. However, after only four years in the league and at the height of his professional superstar career, he walked out of practice one day and quit, never to play again. Why?

He loved being a football player but he hated playing football. He got what he wanted but he hated what he got. He Loved the celebrity perks and fame and fortune that allowed him a successful existence, but because his inner voice and true purpose was misaligned with who he really was and what he did, he would never want what he was getting and would die with his music still in him.

My epiphany: Successful people get what they want, because they 'begin with the end in mind,' which means they focus on a destination of impressive accomplishment, manage people and reward results. However, if we want/need to live a life of significance, we begin with the 'why' in mind, which moves our focus to a journey of important achievement, where we manage expectations and reward effort.

WORK APPLICATION

U.S. national research surveys indicate that 80% of American workers are not working in their dream job. In fact, they admitted they 'hated' their jobs, only looked forward to Friday instead of Monday. Why? They believed they are paid by the hour, when in reality we are all paid for the value we bring to that hour. Can you relate?

Would it be of interest to you to learn how to make our selves more value and irreplaceable?

ONE CLEAR PURPOSE

How would you describe your organizational culture? When you and your coworkers are asked what they do, do they describe the task they perform everyday - or do they energetically describe the purpose of the greater enterprise?

Peter Drucker teaches: "Once we get the culture right, the rest of the stuff takes care of itself." In our millennial 'gig economy' where employees stay in a job for an average of two years, the focus can't just be on attracting and recruiting top talent. We must focus on retaining our best people through personal development programs they won't get from another employer.

We all know some coworkers and teammates who continuously 'suck up' and 'brown nose' their managers and leaders in hopes of getting a raise. However, according to a national Korn Ferry research report, 63% of the 1200 office workers interviewed said they would rather receive a promotion than a raise. The survey reported, "People want to feel that they're contributing to something greater than themselves. They want to see that their work has an impact, and believe a promotion is recognition for their contribution. Regardless if you're a Millennial, GenExer or Baby Boomer, we all value the opportunity to make a difference at our companies over a salary bump. So much for the almighty dollar!

The most interesting part of this research was the fact that 38% of those surveyed expect to be promoted after spending two to three years in a role. In view of the fact that the purpose of a leader is to grow more leaders, is this good or bad? I believe it is good because to be a champion employee and coworker it's what we do when the leader is not around that makes us a champion. Which means when you are a 'Partner Leader' you don't require supervision and can and will make the right decisions when no one else is around!

WHAT ARE YOU COACHING?

Are you trying to coach results or are you coaching behavior? Your answer lies in two follow up inquiries: are you focusing on a "successful" destination, thinking: "when I finally get there or accomplish that I will be impressive?" Or are you enjoying a "significant" journey, knowing what you are doing is important, and that the goal in life is not to "be" this or that - it is to "become" everything you were born to be?

U.S. Armed Forces General Douglas MacArthur said, "If we sweat more in peace, we will bleed less in war." In other words, when practice hurts, games don't. Which obviously inspires every leader to choose the journey of "significance." When you put emphasis on the value of your preparation, training and practice and reward effort, the emphasis automatically shifts from a destination to the journey, which proves true time and again that fully prepared people have no fear and totally inspired people don't have to be motivated!

When you focus on the journey that's important you are still playing to win the game, but you don't focus on the scoreboard. You focus on always and consistently giving your very best effort every play in every way, knowing that when you do, the odds of winning on the scoreboard increase dramatically. In fact, when you focus on The Art Of Significant Leadership and How To Grow People Into Passionate Partners, you start practicing exactly as you play and play as you practice, with absolutely no difference in your level of commitment, speed, hustle and intensity. With this mindset you never just "practice" again. You will always and will only play!

FAMILY APPLICATION

A beautiful, intelligent twenty-year-old young woman is a talented and successful songwriter in Nashville, Tennessee.

Consequently, the lead singing "bad boys of the band" are attracted to her, and she has fallen captive to the celebrity attention. To some fathers this is no big deal.

However, her caring and conservative dad, knowing the probable collateral damage of such fast and furious friendships, has continually counseled her to make sure she knows the end result is tied to the beginning choice.

To his dismay, his fatherly advice fell on deaf ears, and his precious daughter continued to date the prima donnas until her dad spoke from an epiphany he had experienced.

He compared his daughter to a dog chasing cars. If the dog caught the car, what would she do with it? Although she got what she wanted, would she really want what she got? In this "aha moment," his daughter changed her probable future by seeing through a different lens and making a wisely informed choice.

LIFE AND DEATH

During one particularly long, harsh winter, the snowfall in Utah was so deep that it forced the deer population out of the mountains and down into the city parks and residential areas in search of food. Because the deer were stranded, state wildlife agencies immediately brought in truckloads of hay and spread it in the fields around our neighborhood so the deer could eat. One week later more than a hundred dead deer were lying in the streets. Why?

When the veterinarians performed autopsies, they discovered that the stomachs of the deer were full of hay. The deer had eaten plenty of food, but they had not been nourished. They got what they thought they wanted at the moment, but they died because they didn't get what they truly needed.

BEGINNING WITH 'SIGNIFICANCE' IN MIND?

Astronauts who have walked on the moon and mountaineers who have scaled Mt. Everest, who talked mostly of the preparation and exhilarating challenging journey that produced the long-term impact, with only a mere mention of the momentary high they felt when they reached their goal. Which in my world I relate to an American football team who spends the majority of the sixty-minute game strategizing, executing, and working hard to score, but if the players spend more than a few seconds celebrating in the end zone, they are penalized for "excessive celebration."

Because goals are only an excuse for the game – we play the game between the goals – true happiness and authentic lasting fulfillment come primarily from the journey. If the only satisfaction we get from our jobs is a paycheck every two weeks, the forty-hour-work week goes by slowly and emotionally drains us dry.

And as mentioned, if we begin with the end in mind, and put our emphasis on the destination, it oftentimes is a letdown.

When we begin with the 'Significant Why' in mind, we are continually reminded that we are spiritual beings having a physical mortal experience. Which implies that if in fact there is a final judgment when we die, we will not be evaluated and rewarded for the sum total of our good acts - what we have done - and the accumulation of multiple destinations and ends in mind. Rather, we will be blessed and rewarded for who and what we have become because of the journey - not earning our way to heaven, but ending up in heaven because we created heaven on earth!

CHAPTER FOUR

THE FUTURE OF WORK?

"A Lion Is Never Worried About The Opinion Of A Sheep."
The World Has Enough Followers!

In Jacob Morgan's book The Future of Work, he illuminates the many variables in the complex answer to this question, which inspired me to link some of his insights with my research on the future of leadership. His premise matches the premise of the world in the fact that by the time a university student graduates with their degree, the majority of what they learned will be obsolete. Yet, the intriguing thing is that we all have removed ourselves from engaging in any kind of active role in changing this. With the constant blurring of work and life, asking 'what is the future of work' is almost like asking 'what is the future of life?'

For some unidentifiable reason, when we contemplate the future of work we assume that it's something that is going to happen to us – something we need to prepare for and embrace. But what if instead, we turned the question around and asked, 'what is the future of work that we want to create?' Suddenly, we are the proactive players in the game rather than reactive spectators.

Suddenly, we are committed to determine if the future of work will be about AI (Artificial Intelligence) and automation, or about the creation of more socially responsible 'human' companies. Suddenly, we are actively engaged in deciding if technology will create more jobs than it displaces, or if it will displace more jobs than it creates. Surely we cannot allow technology to take over every phase of our lives to where we go to a doctor's office and there is no human being. All we get is a recording that says, "If you have been shot in the head with an arrow please leave your name and number and we'll get back to you in the order of your call. Or if your pain is below the waist press 1." Surely the Catholic Church is not going to automate confessions at "1-800 Fess Up" - with a recording that asks, "If you are into bigamy press 2. If you're worshipping the devil press 666."

To paraphrase Jacob Morgan, "When we decide what the future of work will be like, we realize that technology is simply a tool and why and how and when we use it is a choice." Which means the most effective and efficient leaders will choose to include in their current paradigm an 'old school' Rock Foundational Belief about their role and responsibility as leaders.

THE MOST VALUABLE INTELLIGENCE IS NOT ARTIFICIAL

When we consider the stereotypical role and job description of a leader, his/her responsibilities can be broken down into two major functions: strategy / decision making, and motivating / engaging people. It has already been proven that AI (Artificial Intelligence) can do a better job at analytics and strategy and decision making than a human can. So this part of a leader's responsibility is already obsolete and replaceable. And obviously 'AI' cannot motivate or engage people. Only inspiring people can inspire people to motivate themselves! So in all honesty and transparency, what is the only role left for a leader?

The most amazing and extraordinary, most admired and respected leaders will focus most of their time, energy and talents on just one thing: inspiring his/her people (knowing inspired employees and team members don't have to be motivated), and igniting in others the unique skill sets that only humans possess: passion, creativity, imagination, innovation, complex problem solving, emotional communication, empathy, unconditional love, mutual respect and support, and most significantly, 'being human' – which means we must be Resilient and welcome the opportunities that come from adapting to change.

When a leader triggers in others the use of these powerful attitudes, attributes, character traits and interpersonal communication skills, the leader transforms his/her followers into partners who are equally inspired to also trigger these same qualities in others.

Because leadership 101, as well as management, coaching, teaching, mentoring 101 are couched in the foundational belief: "The only place from which people can grow is where they are," it is crucial that you fully comprehend the different mental, emotional and social 'places' wherein you will find them. Some will be Followers, some Admirers, some Leaders with and without a title, and a few are already interacting as Partners. Knowing this is the only way you can adjust and acquire the necessary tools to become a Significant Partner Leader and figure out the specific role you will play in the future of work.

FOLLOWER, ADMIRER, LEADER, PARTNER, PARTNERSHIP, SIGNIFICANT PARTNER LEADER

A FOLLOWER is defined in the dictionary in two ways: "One who follows the opinions or subscribes to the teachings or imitates the behavior of another." And: "Herd mentality believing there is strength in numbers; timidly going along with the crowd; not personally strong enough to stand up to an opposing popular opinion; content with only going with the flow."

I witnessed an amusing example of the perils found in 'Following' during a trip to my buddy's ranch in Idaho. While we were engaged in a conversation about leadership he asked me to follow him into a corral full of sheep. He placed a rope around the head of one and guided it out of the corral and over to the barn. When I alerted him that the gate was left open he smiled and said, "No worries. They will all follow this sheep and end up following the sheep in front of them and do what it does."

My friend led the sheep to the edge of the barn and directed it to start walking around the outside of the barn in a circular path. Sure enough, every other sheep stepped in line, one by one, nose to tail (bumper to bumper) and followed the sheep in front of it in a single file line that walked around and around the barn.

We left to ride horses for two hours and when we returned, sure enough the sheep were still walking around the barn in the same single file line, following the sheep in front of it. Dogs barked and growled at them and cackling chickens ran by their legs, but the sheep rarely flinched. My buddy laughed and explained the shocking reality that these sheep would continue to walk and follow and walk and follow until they eventually fell over and died of thirst or starvation.

In fact, the weak character (or lack of character) of a sheep is blatantly revealed when it grows its wool to the thickness ready to be shorn and taken to market. In this state, if the sheep accidently slips into water, even shallow water, and its wool becomes water logged and heavy, instead of digging deep to access an inherent spirit to fight or flee and creatively figure out how to get out of the water to survive, the sheep gives up and dies!

Do you know any humans with whom you live and work who epitomize the "Followers" mentality and lack intestinal fortitude like a sheep? Let us never forget the profound quips: "If you are the smartest person in the room, you are in the wrong room." "If everybody in the room is thinking the same, then nobody is really thinking at all." Followers never change the world!

AN ADMIRER never makes any true sacrifices. They always play it safe. Though in words, phrases, songs, they are inexhaustible about how highly they prize the leader, they renounce nothing, give up nothing, will not reconstruct their lives, and most alarming, they will never be what they admire, or let their lives express what it is they supposedly admire. Admirers never change the world!

A LEADER is someone of influence who shows the way as a pioneer, pacesetter, front-runner, skipper, conductor, director, counselor, captain, chieftain, shepherd and/or guide. When someone tells you they became a leader in their organization last week, they really didn't become a leader last week. They were given a leadership title and position, but the position did not make them a leader. Leadership is not a noun - it's an action verb! Appointed leaders never change the world!

A SIGNIFICANT LEADER is someone who stays true to oneself, knowing an original is worth more than a copy. Why escape your intended purpose by copying and trying to be someone else? You will discover who you were meant to be only after you have shown confidence being yourself. For this reason alone, a Significant Leader possesses dazzling 'street smart' social intelligence, a zest for change and continuous improvement, and above all, a vision that allows them to set their sights on the things that truly merit attention.

THE ART OF SIGNIFICANT LEADERSHIP is the capacity to translate a vision into relevant reality by inspiring a common consensus to work and sacrifice toward accomplishing a noble 'Cause.' A noble 'Cause' is a specific movement that is larger than ourselves that motivates us to leave our family, friends, co-workers, teammates, community and world in better shape than we found them.

We know we are becoming a Significant Leader when we share our vision and noble "Cause' and people agree with us and follow us until it becomes a 'Common Cause.' 'Common Cause' is the 'Partner Principle.' Those who are true 'Partners' will stay by our side and work and sacrifice and fight until we achieve the 'Common Cause.' Not because we have a leadership position, but because we subscribe to the leadership truth that John Maxwell calls 'Magnetism' knowing:

"We attract who we are, not who we want.
People do what people see."

A 'PARTNER' is a trusted ally, loyal colleague, consistent collaborator, dependable teammate and courageous 'brother/sister in arms' who is deeply convicted to the core values of duty, honor, integrity, service before self, and a commitment to excellence in all he/she does.

A 'PARTNERSHIP' is an arrangement where parties, known as 'Partners,' agree to cooperate to advance their mutual interests. The partners in a partnership may be individuals, businesses, interest-based organizations, schools, governments or combinations. Organizations may partner to increase the likelihood of each achieving their mission and to amplify their reach. A partnership may result in issuing and holding equity or may be only governed by a contract.

A 'SIGNIFICANT PARTNER LEADER' is best understood in the contrast of a leader who uncovers a personal strength that he/she can do well and who becomes successful at doing/being it; compared to the 'significant leader' who uncovers a personal strength that he/she can do well, who then uses it to do something significant for somebody else that makes a difference; compared to the 'Significant Partner Leader' who uncovers a strength in someone else and helps him/her to become the best version of themselves that he/she was born to be. A 'Significant Partner Leader' has the ability to rally his/her employees and make them excited about moving in the direction that the organization is moving in.

When every individual in any organization firmly believes that he/she is wanted, important and valued as a needed teammate, a 'one for all and all for one' mentality emerges, an understanding that 'when the water in the lake goes up all boats rise together' takes over, and a 'Significant Partner Leadership Culture' is created.

CHAPTER FIVE

AUTHORITY VERSES POWER VERSES LEADERSHIP

"Inspired People Don't Have To Be Motivated"

Many people think that they want Power, and they confuse Authority with Leadership. They fail to comprehend that real powers, effective leadership, and respected authority come not from without, but from within.

Visualize a large convention ballroom filled with 2,500 attendees. You are the keynote speaker at an awards luncheon, standing at the podium with a microphone. You suddenly walk over to the middle of the stage and put a $20-dollar bill on the floor. You ask who wants the money? Many raise their hands but just sit there, hoping you will choose them (typical of life, eh?).

Finally, a man chooses himself, scampers from the third row, and grabs the money. You now ask all of the attendees to interrupt their meals and stand up. Reluctantly everybody slides their desserts to the side and stands. You then tell them to sit down. You pause, and then ask them to stand up again. 95 percent refuse. Why? In two minutes they learned the difference between Authority, Power and Leadership.

AUTHORITY is telling people to do this and that. When you told the audience to stand, they all obeyed you and stood because you were on stage, with a microphone, and in charge. They blindly followed you and sat back down when you told them to. However, when you asked them to again stand, they did not budge because they knew there was no purpose. This validates our authoritarian scenario.

Once our trust and confidence has been violated, we will not follow the authority figure again.

There are many management styles (relationship and task-oriented) and several leadership styles (pragmatic, authoritarian, or servant). They all work to some degree. But it is in the toughest situations and most taxing circumstances of life where the extraordinary leaders emerge.

POWER is something others feel in our presence. Power is not manipulating or controlling, yet many supervisors attempt to force people into positions they are not trained or suited for. And when those people blow it, negative reaction intensifies.

Power comes from within a person within the organization. If the right person is in charge, that person will exercise leadership within the organization only in the context of honorable influence – inspiring by example, opening doors, and providing opportunities for others to become more of who they already are.

Consequently, you can have Power and Authority without Leadership, and Leadership without a Title of Authority and its accompanying Power. True leadership is using influence, not people; setting example, not rules; sharing macro dreams of 'yes,' not micro-managing 'no's'; pulling, not pushing; inspiring, not demanding; communicating, not commanding.

For these reasons, Authority is an elementary use of Power based on a dictatorial mindset where you do what I say "or else!" Leadership is the highest servant mindset where you do what I suggest because I am doing it and setting the example.

LEADERSHIP is not a rank – leadership is not a position. Leadership is a decision – it's a choice and has little to do with your job description in the organization. If you decide to look after the person working to the left of you and serve others to help them grow and become the best version of themselves, you have become a leader!

Leadership is sharing a possibility and inviting people to take advantage of an opportunity - in this case, a chance to get a free twenty-dollar bill. Each of them had to make a decision regarding whether they would sprint to the front. Regardless, it was left up to each of the audience members to choose and act and do something of their own free will and choice.

Free agency is our greatest gift of the universe and choosing to be more, have more, and do more is our greatest responsibility. Leadership is about providing opportunities, direction, and "possibility thinking." It's about asking people if they want to take themselves to the next level. It's about inspiring them to take advantage of the opportunities. It's about instilling in each subordinate a sense of PRIDE: Personal Recognition In Daily Effort.

A true leader teaches correct principles and inspires his/her people to govern themselves. A true leader explains what the task is, sets the expectations, provides training and answers for all involved why they should. Then he/she backs away so the subordinates can use their passion, creativity, imagination and personal motivation to figure out how to "get 'er done!" This in turn transforms them from subordinate followers and admirers into leaders, which welcomes them to join you as Peak Performing Passionate Partners.

ARE YOU A POWERFUL INSPIRATIONAL PARTNER LEADER?

One of my favorite examples of a true 'Partner Leader' is depicted in the historically based movie Spartacus, about a gladiator who led an uprising of slaves against the Roman legions in 71 B.C. For me, the most powerful scene is where Spartacus (played by actor Kirk Douglas) and his slave army had defeated the Romans twice until the general Marcus Crassus finally defeated them. Crassus tells the thousand captured soldiers: "You will die by crucifixion unless you point out to us Spartacus, for we do not know him by sight. If you deliver him to us, we will spare your lives. If not, you will all die."

Spartacus immediately stands up and says, "I am Spartacus." The man next to him also quickly stands and says, "No, I am Spartacus." Another man stands and then another and another until within a minute all thousand men are standing, proclaiming, "I am Spartacus!" Each man, by standing up, chose death. But the loyalty of Spartacus's army was not for Spartacus. Their loyalty was to a shared vision and common 'Cause' that Spartacus inspired - the possibility that they could be free men. This cause was so intoxicating that not even one of the slaves could bear to give up on it and return to captivity.

CHAPTER SIX

"ALL HANDS ON DECK"

"There is no 'I' in Team, but there are two 'Is' in winning – representing:
***I**ndividual preparation ('Don't let me be the weak link') and*
***I**nterdependent collaboration (Making everybody around you better saying, 'I like me best when I'm with you, I want to see you again'). The teams that win have the most 'I' players on them. The organizations that keep winning have the most 'Significant Partner Leaders' on them."*

Being a Significant Partner Leader means that you not only inspire everybody around you like Spartacus by redefining what's possible, but you expect them to do everything in their power to help the team win. WIN means 'What's Important Now,' which obviously could frequently change depending on the task at hand. Using the following metaphorical story about a corporate canoe race, it is easy to see and feel that once an organization gets in the competitive free enterprise race for customers and profitability, every person, regardless of title, tenure, job description, pay grade or official responsibilities, must take ownership, must make winning personal and must be willing to work hard in whatever capacity is required to help the team win.

Although the story is a hypothetical illustration, the reality facts illuminated at its conclusion prove this premise true:

Toyota (a Japanese company) and General Motors (an American company) decided to have a canoe race on the Hudson River. Both teams practiced long and hard to reach their peak performance before the race.

On the big day, the Japanese won by a mile.

The Americans, very discouraged and depressed, decided to investigate the reason for the crushing defeat. A management team made up of senior management was formed to investigate and recommend appropriate action. Their conclusion was the Japanese had 8 people paddling and 1 person steering, while the American team had 7 people steering and 2 people paddling.

Feeling a deeper study was in order, American management hired a consulting company and paid them a large amount of money for a second opinion. They advised, of course, that too many people were steering the boat, while not enough people were paddling.

Not sure of how to utilize that information, but wanting to prevent another loss to the Japanese, the paddling team's management structure was totally reorganized to 4 steering supervisors, 2 area steering superintendents and 1 assistant superintendent steering manager.

They also implemented a new performance system that would give the 2 people paddling the boat greater incentive to work harder. It was called the 'Rowing Team Quality First Program,' with meetings, dinners and free pens for the paddlers. There was discussion of getting new paddles, canoes and other equipment, extra vacation days for practices and bonuses. The pension program was trimmed to 'equal the competition' and some of the resultant savings were channeled into morale boosting programs and teamwork posters.

The next year the Japanese won by two-miles.

Humiliated, the American management laid off one paddler, halted development of a new canoe, sold all the paddles, and cancelled all capital investments for new equipment. The money saved was distributed to the Senior Executives as bonuses.

The next year, try as he might, the lone designated paddler was unable to even finish the race (having no paddles), so he was laid off for unacceptable performance, all canoe equipment was sold and the next year's racing team was out-sourced to India.

The End.

Bottom line Facts: General Motors has spent the last thirty years moving all its factories out of the U.S. claiming they can't make money paying American wages. Toyota has spent the last thirty years building more than a dozen plants inside the U.S. As of 2019, Toyota earned $4 billion dollars in profits while General Motors racked up $9 billion dollars in losses. Hmmm.

And… the General Motors leaders are still scratching their heads and collecting bonuses? If only they knew the difference between leadership as a noun, which is nothing more than a title with power through intimidation and authority with benefits, verses the amazing results and increased profitability that come as a result of creating a Significant Partner Leadership culture.

SIGNIFICANT PARTNER LEADERS EXEMPLIFY CULTURE CREATING TRUTHS

In my over 35 years as a high performance business coach, I have accelerated the growth of thousands of corporations, turned around struggling companies, worked in the merger and acquisition process of amalgamating two organizations into a one heart, one vision, one team culture, and have transformed a last place NFL team into a Super Bowl Champion. In every scenario, I have initiated a cultural transformation by introducing the following seven inner-related, always connected, interdependent, irrefutable truths that translate into 'All Hands On Deck.'

- "Time and Speed Matter! Today you've never been this old before, and today you'll never be this young again. So right now and every right now matters – and age has nothing to do with success or significance - which means no matter what your past has been you have a spotless future – which means you can't always control what happens, but you can always control what happens next! Getting it right the first time is critical to increasing personal and professional productivity.

Acting correctly after it is too late is like sending out wedding invitations after the wedding or locking the door after the house has been robbed!"

- "Everybody must paddle and rise to the occasion to be both a follower and a leader in every situation on every day!"

- "We don't see things as they are – we see things as we are. If we are all looking at the same lashing rainstorm and one complains, 'It's horrible,' and another exclaims, 'It's wonderful,' the weather did not change. What we believe creates our attitude, which creates and sustains our character, which creates and regulates our actions."

- "Self is not discovered – self is created. No, this does not mean you can do anything and be everything. It means you are not perfect, but imperfect – weak and strong - not extraordinary, but ordinary and 'human' with opportunities to do extraordinary things. So is everybody else. Each of us is a work in progress and must commit to being a continuous life-long learner dedicated to always being the best version of our selves. We will make a lousy somebody else!

- "If you wonder if the glass is half empty or half full, you have missed the point. It's Refillable! Thinking positively or negatively doesn't fill up the glass – the pouring does! It's easier to act your way into positive thinking than to think your way into positive action. It's not the sugar that makes the tea sweet, it's the stirring!"

- "We become the average of the five people we associate with the most. If we hang around with five broke people we will become the sixth. If we hang around with five whining, complaining, blaming, “whoa me” people we will become the sixth. When we put a hard to catch horse in the same field with an easy to catch horse, we usually end up with two hard to catch horses. When we put a healthy child in the same room with a sick child, we usually end up with two sick children. In order to become and remain disciplined, healthy and extraordinarily significant we must be willing to pay any price and travel any distance to associate with disciplined, healthy, extraordinarily significant human beings. And yes - in order to attract extraordinary, we must first be extraordinary!”

- “Leading, Selling, Coaching, Teaching, Parenting, Mentoring is the transference of trust.”

By subscribing to and living by these Seven Foundational Truths, your ‘recruiting’ automatically transforms into ‘attracting’ extraordinary people who believe what you believe; which turns your ‘training’ into ‘retaining’ your best people because inspired people don’t have to be motivated. This in turn increases productivity and profitability and improves and sustains high positive morale because everybody from top to bottom and across all departments in your organization believes they are wanted, important, lovable, capable, teachable, needed and engaged in meaningful work for a noble ‘Cause.’

CHAPTER SEVEN

THE RISK OF PURSUING SUCCESS IS THAT YOU MIGHT ACHIEVE IT

"Successful people get what they think they want. Significant individuals want what they get, so they don't die with their music still in them."

SUCCESS FOCUSED LEADERSHIP GURUS MISS THE MARK

In Search of Excellence, first published in 1982, is one of the biggest-selling business books ever, selling three million copies in its first four years and becoming the most widely held library book in the United States from 1989 to 2006. However, author Tom Peters was left wiping egg from his face when many of the firms he profiled quickly proved to be anything but excellent.

In a televised interview, Peters admitted that the book started out as a study of sixty-two companies that he, his coauthor Robert H. Waterman Jr., and some business partners identified as "cool" and doing what they called "cool work." That's it! No science. No quantitative or qualitative common denominators - just their opinions.

OMG! Because these men decided "cool" means "excellent," and they used their influence to sell books, suddenly these so- called "excellent" organizations became the benchmark companies for others to emulate? When the blind lead the blind, don't they both fall into the ditch?

Worse, when the publisher deemed the manuscript too long, Peters and his partners' only criterion to shorten the book was to whittle down their list of sixty-two cool and excellent companies to the forty-three "coolest of the cool." And to show how incompetent, inconceivably crazy, and recklessly irresponsible this exercise was, General Electric, for example, was on the list of sixty-two companies but didn't make the cut to forty-three—which shows you how stupid pure opinion is!

Another business guru debacle was author Gary Hamel's book Leading the Revolution, celebrating the success of Enron and arriving in bookstores as the energy-trading company was blowing up in 2002.

SHOULD HAVE BEEN CALLED "GOOD TO SUCCESSFUL"

And although Jim Collins's book Good to Great was still selling in bookstores in 2019, many of the companies featured were bankrupt and obsolete by 2010—only nine years after its 2001 publication. Why?

Collins defined great companies only as those that sustained market domination for at least fifteen years based on his selected principles of success. Because he focused on principles that are debatable instead of on immutable universal laws that never change, we now know:

"Great is not always good enough, and 'Best' is only relevant depending on what we compare it against"

One can still be evaluated and ranked as the greatest leader/manager in a group of corrupt and dishonest, inefficient, business executives. One can still be recognized as the best parent in a room full of dysfunctional, ineffective, irresponsible mothers and 'deadbeat fathers.' (Any male can be a father, but it takes a special man to be a dad!)

If you play in a charity golf tournament on an 18-hole course with a par of 72, and you shoot 108, and win the tourney because everybody else shoots over 125, that's a bad system! Is it really 'winning' - are you really 'great' and 'best' just because you suck less than your competition sucks? Remember, 'the one eyed man is king in the land of the blind.'

Collins featured Circuit City as "great" in the consumer electronics business, which went bankrupt and out of business and was replaced by Best Buy, which as of 2010 owned 27 percent market share. Collins featured Nokia as the coolest industry leading "Connectivity Company," which is now fourth behind Apple, which launched the iPhone in 2007; Google's Android and the resurgence of Samsung.

In the digital space, Collins showcased Blockbuster and Borders, which are now gone, having been replaced by Netflix and Amazon. And the biggest fiasco and worst example of "great" was Collins's featuring the giant mortgage lender Fannie Mae, which was taken over by the American government to stop it from going bust and taking the global financial system with it.

Yes, all of these examples thrived as successful organizations, but why, in your judgment, did they not live up to the hype and survive as significant?

I would say that most of the things Collins mentioned can be summed up by saying "Great companies make good decisions." Hiring the right people? That describes a company that makes good hiring decisions. Confronting brutal facts? That is an important part of the process of making good decisions.

Collins's team looked at the companies that went from good to great and asked, "What do all these have in common?" But they never went back and asked, "Are there any companies that have these traits that did not make the leap from good to great?

Lest you think we are the only organization out there unimpressed by Good to Great, check out Wharton's review: "Collins asks an interesting question. Unhappily, the methodology he used to formulate an answer is questionable, and the answer is almost disappointing in its simplicity: Great companies become great by staying focused on their products, their customers, and their businesses, with an organization-al culture that embraces constant change. That's the book." It should have been called Good to Successful.

Bottom line. Are you strong or weak, tall or short, wide or thin, fast or slow, smart or stupid, pretty or pretty ugly? Says who? Compared to what? Answer: you are beautiful and strong and smart and amazing just the way you are!

Albert Einstein said, "Everybody is a genius. But if you judge a fish by its ability to climb a tree it will spend its whole life believing it is stupid."

The only way we can ever become the very best versions of our selves - personally and organizationally - is to stop competing against others and focus on the fact that the only person and organization that we need to be better than is the person and organization we were yesterday!

Successful organizations share certain positive attributes, but when they also share the cancerous qualities and convoluted mindsets of unsuccessful organizations, they too, will eventually fall by the wayside.

What have been some of the convoluted mindsets of organizations you're aware of? (Consider red tape bureaucracy, seniority entitlement, "we are the competition" complacency, and so forth.)

What does your experience and wisdom tell you are the cancerous qualities of organizations? (Consider staying in "silos," possessiveness of information, jealousy of others, gossip, and so forth.

What are the convoluted mindsets and cancerous qualities in your organization?

Contrary to popular belief, the organizations that were highlighted in good to great and that ultimately fail did not suffer their demise because they didn't have a charismatic leader. Three of the most charismatic leaders of the twenty-first century were, Stalin of Russia, Hitler of Germany and Saddam Hussein of Iraq. However, they were also self-centered dictators focused on acquiring individual power and glory, who as murdering thugs caused the suffering of millions. Clearly they are three of history's worst examples of the antithesis of collaborative Partner Leadership.

Neither was the demise of these "good to great" organizations caused because the corporate leaders lacked innovation and refused to invest in the latest IT digital advancements and high-tech gizmos and gadgets. They ultimately failed because the leaders didn't look high and far enough into the future or drill deep enough into their "organizational soul" to realize that there is a level beyond success that keeps their value proposition relevant and both their internal and external customers feeling fulfilled and needed. The following questionnaire will allow you to evaluate yourselves and better execute with your internal and external customers:

"P P I"
PERSONAL PROGRESS INTERVIEW

- What is your personal unique ability or characteristic that sets you apart from everyone else?
- What is your organization's unique ability?
- What are your personal strengths that make you successful?
- What are your organization's strengths that make it successful?
- What are the opportunities that you can pursue right now and for the next ninety days?
- What are the opportunities your organization can pursue for the next ninety days?
- What are the immediate, urgent, short-term, and long-term challenges that you face in achieving your personal goals?
- What are the threats and obstacles to achieving your organization's goals?
- When will you know you are successful - personally and professionally?
- When will your organization be considered successful and 'significant'?
- Who have you inspired today that will leave you, saying, "I like me best when I'm with you, I want to see you again?"

CHAPTER EIGHT

THE FOUNDATIONAL SIGNIFICANCE OF FINDING YOUR 'WHY'

"The two most important days in your life are the day you are born and the day you find out why." — Mark Twain

One day during my American football practice session, the coach whistled: "go," and another player and I ran full speed into each other to practice our tackling technique. After a brutal head-on collision, I lay on the ground in shock, with a sharp, piercing pain shooting through my body. My eye drooped and my speech slurred (which momentarily returned). I had compressed my neck, severed the axillary nerve in my right deltoid, and suffered a grade-2 concussion.

By nightfall my neck was stiff, my right side was numb, my arm dangled by my side, and I perspired profusely, shook, and threw up until I cried myself to sleep.

For the next fourteen months I was paralyzed—both physically and emotionally. My heart was broken, my dreams were shattered, and my successful and promising life came crashing down.

Now that I've recovered, I'm often asked what took so long? Simply: I kept asking the wrong questions. I was asking the doctors how to get better when I should have been asking myself, "Why?" As soon as I answered the "why" and felt the "want," figuring out the "what" and "how to" was simple.

Once I stopped focusing on having fame and chasing fortune and started focusing on achieving my real purpose and becoming whole, I was able to persevere the pain of rehabilitation and do the hard things required to become everything I was really born to be.

Because adversity introduces us to ourselves, I am the man I am and have the perspective that I have because of this ordeal. And through it all, I learned, "When we do today what others won't, we will accomplish tomorrow what others can't, turn our stumbling blocks into stepping stones, and transform our setbacks into come backs.

THE BIOLOGY OF THE BRAIN

The 'why I do what I do' and my wanting to do it exist in the limbic part of the brain that controls my feelings and decision-making.

What to do and how to do it exist in the neo-cortex part of the brain that controls my rational thought and my language.

A clearly defined 'why' coupled with a compelling 'want' (goal) have a gigantic impact on behavior because they engage more than simply the brain. They also engage the heart. Research proves that a clear, concise, personally meaningful and challenging goal causes our blood to pump more rapidly, our brain to fire, and our muscles to engage.

When I have only a 'what' and a 'how' without a 'why' and a 'want', no such effects take place.

Limbic system structures control my emotions and motivations, including fear, anger, excitement, joy; my inherent desire for continuous progress; my survival instincts and my long-term memory, deter-mined by how much emotional response an event invokes.

The **Neo-cortex** is involved in higher functions such as sensory perception, generation of motor commands, spatial reasoning, conscious thought, and language.

Notice that the decision-making (why) and feeling (want) function of the brain reside in a completely different place than the rational thought (what) and language (how) function of the brain. This is why it is oftentimes difficult to explain why you buy something or do something simply because it "feels right."

THE PSYCHOLOGY OF THE BRAIN

I must know why I do what I do because I can't motivate myself and inspire others with just what I do. I must be able to articulate why I exist and the purpose of every task I am asked to perform. Why is the source of my ambition and motivation and the emotional fuel that drives me to want to adhere to all Twelve Highest Universal Laws.

THE SOCIOLOGY OF THE BRAIN

Starting with why puts focus on my journey. But for my why to survive, it needs the structure of what and how and a destination of where and when, which means I must also "keep" the end in mind.

Magnifying your 'why' comes through passion, generated when you make your reason for doing extremely personal. Which means your why must also include beginning with You in mind! When you begin with You in mind, you see the journey as the goal and make You the actual End in mind.

Remember, the purpose of life is not just to be—it is to constantly become. Which means nothing happens to you—everything happens for you, to tutor you during your journey toward reaching your ultimate capacity and potential as a human being.

BEGIN WITH THE "WHY" IN MIND – BEGIN WITH YOU IN MIND

For the record, I am a strong believer in a Supreme Being. However, recovering from an injury and overcoming enormous odds is usually not a miracle. It is because of obedience to two specific universal laws:

One is the law of the harvest: when you plant wheat, you get wheat; when you plant expectations, purpose, hard work, and clear consequences, you get desired results.

The other law, which also works in business and the military, is Sigmund Freud's famous Law of "Sublimation." Freud taught that because all power is in the subconscious, and pain in the subconscious is the cause of our failures, the way we combat these premises in our world of survival of the fittest, is by simply taking pain, anger, frustration, and disappointment and using them as fuel to succeed. In other words, pain is the secret to achievement. My fourteen months long recovery from my paralyzing football injury validates this truth, which consequently inspires me to remind the world to always begin with the "why" in mind.

CHAPTER NINE

WHY AND WHAT DETERMINE YOUR WHEN AND HOW

"The eyes of vision are useless when the mind is blind. The hands of service are useless when the heart is cold. The ears of learning are useless when the conscience is deaf. The connection with heaven is useless when the spirit is dead."

For a minute, believe that you have agreed to participate in an intense experiment where a large truck pulls up in front of your home and unloads a 200-foot (61-meter) steal I beam onto the road. You are asked to stand on one end of the beam while a facilitator stands at the other end of the beam. He asks if you will walk across the 200-foot beam, without touching the ground, for a free 100-dollar bill? If you fall off, you don't get the money. Will you go across? Yes.

You are now invited to accompany the facilitator to Malaysia, where a large crane has lifted this 200-foot steal I beam to the top of the famous PETRONAS Twin Towers in Kuala Lumpur—one of the tallest buildings in the world, standing 88 stories tall (1,483 feet high or 452 meters), and has positioned the beam to connect the two towers, which are 190 feet (58 meters) apart.

You are now asked to stand on the top of one tower while the facilitator is on the top of the other tower, where he asks if you will still walk across the 200-foot beam to receive a free 100-dollar bill? (Because at this height the crosswind is usually blowing at around 30 miles per hour and the humidity in the air makes the beam extra slippery, most would answer “no.” And if you fall off you don’t get the money). Will you walk across for one thousand dollars? No? Will you walk across for one million dollars?

Suddenly the facilitator brings your beautiful eight-year-old daughter to the edge of the building with the threat that if you don’t walk across the beam to save her, he will drop her to her death. Would you now go across?

Of course you would walk across the beam—we all would! What are the three “whys” revealed in this scenario?

When the beam was in front of your home securely on the ground, you willingly walked across it because money mattered most to you.

When the beam was taken to the top of the PETRONAS Towers, you refused to walk across because your personal safety mattered most.

However, when the facilitator threatened to drop your daughter unless you walked across to save her, you willingly walked across the beam because of the love you have for your beautiful daughter, which is more important and significant than money or your personal safety.

Bottom line: What matters most is what lasts the longest. True love inspires us to rise to any occasion to serve someone, and it motivates us to take the required immediate action to even save someone, more quickly than any other influence in the world.

"KEEPING" YOU AS THE END IN MIND

Focusing on purpose and our love of accomplishing what matters most at the moment also unleashes our passion, creativity and imagination, which is at the heart and soul of innovation and perseverance. To illustrate invite you to presuppose that today is Monday and you were just notified that you won a million dollars in a contest and must be at the designated office to pick up your check at precisely 5 p.m. on Friday, four days from today.

Excitedly you promise you will be there, write down the address, and immediately go to Map Quest to figure out your GPS-guided route and the projected drive time to your destination. You discover it is 120 miles away and will take you approximately two hours to get there. When will you leave? You laugh and excitedly scream, "Right now!"

Obviously you can't leave until Friday, but you make arrangements at work to leave at 1:30 p.m. to give yourself enough extra time in case there is traffic or an unexpected accident. You depart on schedule, but within five minutes after you merge onto the interstate, all traffic suddenly comes to a screeching halt. You are on a four-lane highway, and every car is stopped in front of you and behind you in every lane on both sides of the interstate.

After sitting patiently for twenty minutes, you finally get out of your car and walk until you discover there has been a brutal crash with a fatality, involving three eighteen-wheel tractor/trailer truck hauling giant logs to a paper mill. Not only have the mangled trucks blocked all lanes of traffic, but also the huge logs have been scattered across the highway in every direction, which will require a crane to be brought in to begin clearing away the debris. Official news is that the entire highway in both directions will be closed for at least four hours.

It is now 2 p.m. with a two-hour drive still ahead of you, and if you don't show up on time, you don't get the money. Will you just sit there, give up on this once-in-a-lifetime opportunity, and blame your circumstances, which are supposedly "out of your control," claiming, "There was nothing I could do to accomplish this dream goal?" Or will you still arrive at your destination at 5 p.m. to receive your mil-lion-dollar check?

Because "necessity is the mother of invention," would you willingly leave your car, find a motorcycle rider, and offer to buy the motorcycle on the spot for $70,000 so you could ride and weave it through the scattered debris to arrive on time? Or would you pull out your cell phone, call a helicopter company, and willingly pay the $70,000 for them to pick you up in an adjoining field and fly you to your appointment on time?

Bottom line: When your "why" includes you as the end in mind, you become more passionate, creative, imaginative, resourceful and motivated to turn your patience into perseverance and not let what you cannot do interfere with what you can do, especially in becoming everything you were born to be!

MUST WE BECOME SUCCESSFUL TO BE SIGNIFICANT?

Because answering "why" literally moves you from a focus on achieving success to a higher mindset and heart-set of experiencing significance, the answer is a resounding yes!

Yes, you must first be successful before you can become significant! You must know and experience what impressive success is before you are in a position to compare and contrast it to the deep feelings of being important and significant.

Anybody can be Significant. For example, in 2006, at Greece Athena High School in Rochester, New York, USA, a young man named Jason McElwain, was serving the basketball coach as team manager, responsible for the balls and bringing water to the players at practice and wiping the sweat off their faces during games. Most interesting to the story is that Jason, nicknamed J–Mac, had been diagnosed with 'Autism' as a two-year-old boy.

Consequently, because of his year long dedication to the team, before the final game of the season, Jason was presented with his own team uniform with his name on the back of the jersey and invited to sit on the bench as part of the team.

It was the final game of the season between two arch rival schools. The gymnasium was packed with screaming fans and families cheering on their friends, sons, brothers and favorite team. Obviously a coach is hired to win games and oftentimes his/her job security is based on successfully winning the championship.

However in this particular game, this coach – Coach Jim Johnson, decided he would teach his players and his fans what it means to achieve the level beyond success – and practice the Art of Significant Leadership.

With four minutes left in the game, Coach Johnson called time out and put Jason in the game. His teammates stood and cheered and the hometown crowd screamed and chanted his name! As his teammate dribbled the ball up the floor, he passed it to Jason who shot and scored a short two point shot. But where the story really gets unbelievably inspirational and exciting is on the next time down the court when Jason launched a long three point shot. Swish! He scores! And his teammates and fans go crazy!

The next time up the floor his teammate again passed him the ball, and again Jason launched a three-point shot! Swish! He scored again, and his teammates and school fans continued to stand and cheer! And yes, the next time he caught a pass he launched an even longer three point shot that swished and scored! Three in a row!

However, this time the opposing team members and coaches and the rival school fans stood and cheered and joined in chanting his name, transforming the entire gym into a frenzy of appreciation! Not to be denied, the next three times up the court Jason shot three more three pointers that swished and scored! That's six three-point shots that he made in a row – the last one from way out with only three seconds left in the game!

Jason had scored 20 points in just 4 minutes and was the leading scorer in the entire game! As the game ended both teams rushed onto the floor to give Jason 'high fives!' There wasn't a dry eye in the gym as they lifted him onto their shoulders and carried him around to the cheers of everyone there. Guaranteed not one person looked at the scoreboard and to this day would not be able to tell you the final score of the game.

It didn't matter. In just four minutes at the end of a high school basketball game, this amazing and inspirational basketball Coach Johnson taught his players and fans and the other team's players and fans the magnificent difference between accomplishing success and being Significant.

SIGNIFICANCE MUST BE PERSONAL

In another American high school athletic competition at Wasatch High in Heber Utah, an eighteen-year-old wrestler was going into the final meet of the regular season. He had already won enough matches to be crowned the regional champion and qualify for the State Wrestling Tournament.

This meant his final match meant nothing. Ironically, it was against a young man with Down syndrome who had been pinned in the first thirty seconds of every one of his previous twelve matches. The champ could win this match with his eyes closed!

However, as soon as the referee said, "wrestle," this special needs athlete floored the champ in a single leg takedown and then turned him on his back in some sort of broncobuster, butterfly Granby move—holding him in a cradle to pin him. The crowd leaped to their feet in astonishment!

The champ escaped, of course, but only to be captured again and put in another exotic WWE figure-four-leg lock that no one had ever seen before! The crowd roared even louder! Again the champ escaped, only to be taken down again as the two athletes rolled and flipped and traded moves for the rest of that minute.

At the end of the third period, with the clock ticking down the final seconds of the match, the champ was flipped onto his back and pinned. The young man with Down syndrome jumped to his feet, and with a gigantic smile, he jumped up and down until the referee raised his hand in victory. There wasn't a dry eye in the gym!

As the regional champ hugged him and his teammates carried him on a victory lap around the mat, it was obvious to everyone that this match really did mean something to the champ. Both had won.

With no encouragement from his coach or parents, this champion made sure the match went the distance. And in less than six minutes, he had taught everyone that success is being one in the world. Significance is being the world to one!

BOTTOM LINE

Living a life of Significance and achieving the level beyond success begins and never ends when we focus of purpose instead of just setting goals. Jim Rohn said, "Life responds to deserve and not to need. It doesn't say, 'If you need, you will reap.' It says, 'If you plant, you will reap.' And the single most important thing that we can plant is a clearer understanding of the purpose of every action and reaction in life that up-levels and upgrades our personal truth.

Remember, the so-called leaders who only have a title and some power and authority act like 'travel agents' trying to send people to places they have never been. However, Significant Partner Leaders are 'travel guides' who have earned the right and respect and belief of their people to take them where they want to go because they have already been there themselves - not just physically, spiritually, and emotionally, but philosophically in their deep comprehension of the purpose of everything!

CHAPTER TEN

WHEN YOU KNOW THE LAWS OF THE UNIVERSE YOU CAN FORECAST YOUR DESTINY

We all start our lives doing what is necessary to get what we want, but oftentimes we end up in a completely different physical and emotional place than where we thought we would be—and we don't want what we got. It's like the pilot who took off from an airport at the equator, intending to circumnavigate the globe.

But because his course was off by just one degree, by the time he re-turned to the same longitude, he was lost. An error of only one degree put him almost 500 miles (800 km) off course, where he crash-landed after running out of fuel.

No one wants life to end in an unintended place—a destination of meaningless selfishness or in a crash caused by regrets. But all too often, as pilots of our destinies and captains of our souls, we set out on what we hope will be a successful journey only to realize too late that an error of a few degrees has set us on a course of significant disaster.

The bad news is that most of us who discover we are off course think we can change immediately. This is true to some degree, in that we can stop going in the wrong direction the second we discover it. But in an analogy from the world of physical fitness, we don't go to the gym once and leave a changed man or woman in the best shape of our lives.

The good news is that fitness comes in daily doses through obedience to a disciplined regimen over time, not in binges. So does personal development and Significant Partner Leadership prowess.

Too many leaders are put through a workshop, being trained like a weekend warrior, instead of being coached and conditioned like an elite athlete and being pushed and pulled through a rigorous pro-gram - growing, developing, and being strengthened one day at a time over a calculated period of continuous improvement.

In the context of our study of universal laws, when we know and subscribe to the laws, we can always begin our journey on the right course, correct our course if we get off track, and maintain our daily continuous improvement regimen until we reach our predetermined goal. In the grand scheme of things, universal laws, also referred to as the laws of nature, are the unwavering and unchanging laws that govern every aspect of the universe and are the means by which our world and the entire cosmos continue to exist, thrive, and expand.

THERE IS AN ORDER IN THE UNIVERSE

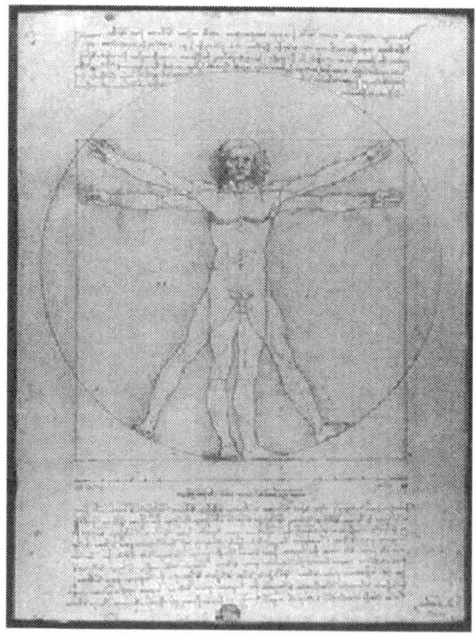

The Vitruvian Man is a drawing created by Leonardo da Vinci circa 1490 that depicts a male figure in two superimposed positions with his arms and legs apart and simultaneously inscribed in a circle and square. The drawing is based on the correlations of ideal human pro-portions with geometry, showcasing Leonardo's understanding of the direct correlation of man to nature, which are also analogous to the workings of the universe.

Da Vinci's sketch of the essential symmetry of the human body is, by extension, a symbol of the evidence of law and order found in the universe as a whole.

To da Vinci and the other thought-leading mathematicians, philosophers, artists, architects, musicians, and scientists that came before him and certainly after him up to this day, it is obvious that there was a specific mathematical formula used in the organization of the Universe, in the creation of the human race, and even in the design of beauty, driven by proportion and governed in a disciplined, interactive, interdependent order shown even in the symmetry of leaves and the geometric perfection of snowflakes.

When we observe our world in the context of the art and science of the earth's ecosystem and the complex relationship among our brain, mind, and body, and how this affects human behavior, da Vinci's revelation is true and clear. Mother Nature is not unpredictable, and the order in the universe repeats itself over and over again in every aspect of our existence, producing predictable results, which the unaware still call random occurrence, coincidence, or luck.

DAN SOARS TO THE EDGE OF SPACE

I became blatantly aware of this on October 23, 2010, when I had the rare opportunity to soar to the edge of space in a U2 Reconnaissance Aircraft:

(YouTubedanclarku2spyplane). Because it was a classified mission, I can only tell you that at 70,000 feet you can see two-thirds of the state of California. At 80,000 feet you see mapped outlines of America. And at 90,000 feet you tear up and realize that if mortality is all there is, what a waste this life will be!

In a sortie that lasted four hours, I sat in the sounds of silence looking at the breathtaking curvature of the earth, gazing into the endless blackness of space, experiencing an unobstructed view of the universe, and with a sixteen-mile high perspective on life and leadership, I realized that we are all interconnected in a world governed by a specific set of universal laws.

My epiphany: When I found the place inside myself where nothing is impossible, I realized there is a level beyond success available to those who realize that acquiring wealth, having authority, and gaining popularity through accomplishments that make a living and endure only while we are alive are meaningless unless we also achieve the significance of love, admiration, loyalty, respect, and relevance through accomplishments that make a difference and endure even beyond the grave. I now know the goal is not to live forever. The goal is to create something that will.

Clearly I could see that all of humanity is actually a family of brothers and sisters realizing that the same God who made me, made everybody else, too. I could see that we all live on the same Mother earth as interdependent, inter-connected partners realizing that it is not my air - it is our air. It is not my water - it is our water. Tragically, I could see that all borders that divide countries and segregate ethnic populations and create wars that kill people in the name of a particular religious' tradition are manmade and not part of the original master plan of creation.

Although I could see the earth is round, it became clear that the world is metaphorically 'flat' and small and accessible and better served and protected when every one of us in every country partner to make the world safe, loving, forgiving and prosperous for all.

SCIENTIFIC EVIDENCE

Werner von Braun was a German, later American, aerospace engineer and space architect credited with inventing the Saturn V rocket for the United States and being the father of rocket technology and space science in America. Following World War II Werner served as director of the newly formed Marshal Space Flight Center and developed the rockets that launched the United States' first space satellite Explorer 1, and the Apollo program manned lunar landings.

The dictionary defines science as: "the intellectual and practical activity encompassing the systematic study of the structure and behavior of the physical and natural world through observation and experiment." Logic and reason and proof of concept are the things that keep scientists up at night and curious all day! As one of the most celebrated scientists and mathematicians of all time with one of the most brilliant minds on the planet, von Braun concluded, "that the world of technology and the world of science and chemistry, which gave us our fantastic insights into the atoms and the stars, and even into the mysteries of live organisms - must somehow fit into the design of a greater system in which our human destiny, too, finds its place and its meaning.

Von Braun concluded, "There are specific mathematical equations and algorithms that must be correctly calculated and used in order to put a man into space and bring him back to earth through the earth's atmosphere safely. Consequently, it is obvious that we live in a world in which a fantastic amount of logic and rational lawfulness is at work. We are aware of a large number of laws of physics and chemistry and biology which, by their mutual interdependence, make nature work as if it were following a grandiose plan from its earliest beginnings to the farthest reaches of its future destiny."

SPACE TRAVEL IS POSSIBLE ONLY BECAUSE WE OBEY SPECIFIC RULES AND LAWS

The blockbuster movie Hidden Figures is a true story about an African American woman named Katherine Johnson, who landed a job at NASA and became a national hero. The film illuminates astronaut John Glenn's historic flight in the Mercury spacecraft, and why his mission of orbiting the earth three times single-handedly launched our space program into what it is today.

One key question that was baffling everyone was calculating the exact position over the Earth to fire the retrorockets in order to land in the center of the ocean recovery zone. Katherine was the one who came up with the solution!

During a pivotal scene, Johnson and a team of white, male engineers are staring at a chalkboard, trying to solve equations for the trajectory of astronaut John Glenn's space capsule. They're stumped until Johnson hits upon a solution: "Euler's Method," she says. "That's ancient," says one of the engineers incredulously. "Yes. But it works and has always worked," she counters. "It works numerically."

FYI - Euler's Method was developed by Swiss mathematician Leonhard Euler (1707-1783), and tackles a common challenge where a 'Differential Equation' can't be solved exactly, so mathematicians must figure out ways to approximate the answers for specific situations – especially in physics problems that describe the path of a moving object subject to changing gravitational forces. The only way Euler's Method works is to fully understand the intricate orderly organization of the universe and how one never changing, always present law interfaces with another law that must be obeyed to achieve a specific result.

CHAPTER ELEVEN

HOW THE UNIVERSE OPERATES

The universe was organized and is governed by a set of irrevocable laws. The highest law is Obedience. All other laws, rules and principles are governed by it and subject to it. When you obey a specific law, you reap a specific reward and response that conform to that obedient action. When you disobey a specific law, you realize and suffer a specific consequence to that action of disobedience.

OBEDIENCE

For this reason, the Law of Practicing Obedience transcends gender, age, tenure, race, and every socioeconomic condition. Sometimes we are tempted to measure our progress by looking at what others are choosing to obey, do, or have achieved. But your path is unique to you. If you choose to take detours, then you and only you can find your way back.

No one is exempt from obeying the highest universal laws. Neither are any of us allowed to selectively obey without suffering the con-sequences of disobedience just because we are older, seasoned, more experienced veterans who think we are above and beyond the law.

FREEWILL AGENCY

To test our obedience, we were given "Freewill Agency." In order to create our own life experiences, we were given our freewill agency so that we might constantly exercise this gift while living on this planet governed by the universal laws. Because the Law of Practicing

Obedience is the first law of the universe and is always constant, our agency allows us in every situation to choose to either be obedient to those laws or not to be obedient.

OPPOSITION IN ALL THINGS

In order to guarantee our agency, the world was also organized with at least two or more choices in every aspect of our existence that are related, opposite, contrary, corresponding, or radically different:

- Without darkness, we don't appreciate light.
- Without falsehood, we cannot cherish truth.
- Without justice, there can be no mercy.
- Without death, life is not sacred and honored.
- Without agency and opposition, there are no options and we could not be enticed by one or the other.

CONSCIENCE

To help us with our choices, we were given an inherent ability at birth to discern right from wrong, truth from falsehood, and good from evil. We commonly call this natural ethical intuition our conscience. Because every human being is born with a conscience, our conscience will never fail us. Only our desire to follow it decreases as we continue to make bad choices and do the wrong thing.

Thus, freewill isn't quite as "free" as it seems - at least not from the point of view of significance. Without agency, we could not choose rightly and progress; yet with agency we can choose wrongly and fall short of our potential as a human being.

Because of the way some use their agency they lose their agency. When we don't obey universal laws or the specific rules that derive from them, our opportunities are reduced, and we fall captive to our choices. However, when we do obey, our obedience ultimately protects our agency.

Herein lies the deepest truth: Obedience does not replace freewill agency. Agency is still the greatest gift of the universe. But if we feel compelled and coerced by leaders to obey, we are merely obeying the leader instead of the law and will never reap the full promised and correlating increase and reward attached to that specific law.

When your why is not our own, our how will always be halfhearted and incomplete. However, when we are humble and free of stubbornness of heart, and we choose to obey without being compelled to be humble and obedient, we will always reap the full measure of the specific reward and increase attached to that obedience.

CONTROLING YOUR DESTINY

When you choose to align, obey, and harmonize with the highest laws of the universe in a conscious and intentional way, you seize control of your destiny by finding your flow in every aspect of your life— whether physically, mentally, financially, relationally, emotionally, or spiritually, and you create the life you need.

The challenge is that the vast majority of the world doesn't comprehend this and believes that life just happens as it will.

Most people have developed a predominant way of thinking, acting, and doing that causes them to overlook the obvious simplicity of the process of creation that comes by consciously and purposefully obeying universal laws.

They perceive that the various events, conditions, and circumstances we all experience in life are just a random series of occurrences, believing that there is no definitive purpose or underlying reason that things happen as they do.

Because most people believe everything is just "meant to be," they continue to struggle long and hard, choosing to swim against rather than with the flow of life. As a result, they continue to experience limited, mediocre, and at best hard-earned and temporary results.

They attempt to seek and find happiness and fulfillment through external means, such as working more hours and accumulating more material things, which does nothing more than create physical fatigue, mental burnout, emotional exhaustion, anxiety, fear, disappointment, discouragement, doubt, worry, and a host of other counterproductive effects that serve only to create precisely the opposite of the outcome desired.

For this reason, you must deepen your understanding and heighten your awareness of why and how these universal laws operate as they do and what your level of engagement needs to be.

IT'S ABOUT "BEING" MORE THAN "DOING"

Because these laws have always existed and always will, your job is more about "being" than it is about "doing," which is precisely why so many "do" so much and experience such limited results.

Your job is to clearly define the why and the what. The job of each universal law is to provide the when and the how. Universal laws al-ways do their job, and the more intentional, focused, and consistent you are in doing your part, the quicker universal laws do theirs.

The laws that govern every aspect of existence and that are responsible for determining your individual life as well as every event, condition, and circumstance in the universe, operate with the same precise, predictable, and unwavering certainty, regardless of your age, race, creed, geographical location, education, gender, religion, or socioeconomic condition.

The only thing that determines how they work in your life and what is created as a result of their perfect and unfailing operation is your total understanding that you possess the power and the ability to be, do, and have the life you dream of, based only upon your choosing.

Every significant corporate executive, military leader, educator, and athletic coach can quote Goethe's words: "When we treat a man as he is, we make him worse than he is; but when we treat him as if he is already what he potentially could be, he becomes what he should be." Einstein explained: "Everybody is a genius. But if you judge a fish by its ability to climb a tree, it will live its whole life believing that it is stupid."

For these reasons, let us stop letting what we cannot do interfere with what we can do, and start becoming everything we were born to be: physically, mentally, spiritually, emotionally, financially, and socially, and in our families.

No more misjudging the extent of our potential. And rather than compare ourselves with others, let us compete with ourselves, for we all will make a lousy somebody else.

Remember, the difference between a significant individual and a successful person is that the significant individual will do what the successful person will not do.

The kicker is: oftentimes the significant individual doesn't want to do it either, but he/she does it anyway!

The key, then, is to take what we know and apply it to what we want to achieve and who we want to become - especially when it comes to appreciating the value of human life. Because we are all interconnected, if each person concentrated solely on mastering every phase of himself or herself—particularly our thoughts, words, and deeds—we would not have time to think negatively about anyone else and would actually accelerate becoming the complete person we have the potential to be!

CHAPTER TWELVE

INTERFACING WITH THE UNIVERSE

"PARABLE OF THE KITE"

The orderly organization of the universe and how we most effectively and efficiently interface with it by following the rules of engagement, is best explained in my 'Parable of the Kite.'

Dad and his young son are in a park flying a kite. Dad asks him what holds the kite up in the sky. The boy answers, "The wind." Dad explains, "No, the string holds the kite up in the sky." Confused, the boy argues, "No, the string holds the kite down." Smiling, Dad says, "If you think so, let go of the string."

Obviously, when the boy let go of the string, the kite fell from the sky. As the wind blew the kite wherever it decided to, the boy chased the string until he caught it. When he grabbed hold of the string, the kite again climbed skyward to be everything it was meant to be and do everything it was meant to do at the highest level possible.

In this scenario **The Kite** represents his (your) desired results - high expectations, goals, specific calculated increase, and wanted or needed extraordinary outcomes.

The Wind represents opposition - the economy, interest rates, competition, lack of capital investment, negative co-workers, death of a loved one, loss of a job, a devastating divorce, Post Traumatic Stress, and the causes of suicide, including debt, infidelity, alcohol, drugs, and untreated depression.

The String represents the Twelve Highest Universal Laws, as well as every preparatory success principle, core value, and rule that he (you) must follow in order to achieve the desired result.

The boy **Holding Tightly To The String** represents his (your) personal commitment to resist the "opposition" and take control of his desired result through obedience to the specific law that allows him to reap a specific reward. Holding the string also represents him obeying his dad (you obeying a boss, coach, teacher, Bishop, Mission President, person in authority) out of expectation, not out of freewill choice.

The boy **Letting Go of the String** represents him (you) succumbing to the enticements of others and experiencing the consequence of disobedience as he watched the kite blow away.

The boy **Chasing the String** represents him (you) following his conscience and realizing that he had disobeyed a specific law and needed to immediately obey it again.

The boy **Once Again Holding Tightly To The String** represents his (your) realization that you should never obey a person, because they will eventually let you down. Because he now has firsthand experience in suffering the consequences of disobedience, he decides to exercise his free will agency and chooses only to obey the law—not because it's expected by his dad, but because it's demanded of himself. Which means he no longer has to fly his kite with the supervision of his dad.

And when a friend or family member tries to **Tempt Him (you) Into Letting Go Of The String** he realizes he/she is a bad influence; when a friend, co-worker, teammate, associate, fellow missionary attempts to coerce you into breaking the rules/ disobey the highest laws, you now know he/she is a bad influence and you should steer clear of the negativity!

As the force of the air blows against the face of the kite, and as you hold onto the string, you create an equal and opposite force against the wind, and this force allows the kite to climb. If you disobey this law of opposition by letting go of the string, the kite does not fly.

Ultimately, when you refuse to obey and decide to let go of the string, the wind of opposition blows your kite (goal) anywhere it chooses, eventually leading it to its demise. Only when you obey the highest laws can you withstand and resist your natural carnal tendencies and temptations, cage your materialistic appetites, circumvent your selfish motivations, regain control of your finances, reestablish your loving relationships, and achieve the Level Beyond Success.

If you merely drift through life and allow the winds of change to take you wherever they choose, thinking freewill gives you the ability to do so, life will pay you its own price, on its own terms. But the kite flyer who exercises his agency properly makes life pay on his own terms on your terms!

CHAPTER THIRTEEN

CATEGORIES OF UNIVERSAL LAWS

NON-EXISTENT LAWS THAT ARE HUMAN FABRICATIONS

Luck: Sometimes we are so ignorant of the laws that we attribute what happens to us not to law but to luck. In reality, nature knows no such law as luck. Do you agree?

Coincidence: This occurs when the laws of attraction, harvest, and learning simultaneously interface. Have you ever experienced this?

Entitlement: This is something we think we deserve but didn't pay a personal price to obtain. Do some leaders or team members in your organization or citizens in your community or country think they are entitled to certain things just because they work there or live there? Why?

A government that overtaxes its contributing citizens to subsidize its noncontributing residents eventually implodes—parasites (big government and a welfare state) that live off the host (tax-paying citizens) eventually always kill the host!

It is NOT 'politically incorrect' to state that living in America does not make someone an American! The truth is: America is more than a landmass with amazing natural resources. It's an experiment in self government founded on a set of specific ideals and perpetuated on timeless principles that we believe are God-given 'inalienable rights.'

On September 11, 2001, nineteen fanatical terrorists did not attack a country. They attacked what we believe in. To be an American means you believe in our Constitution and in our Declaration of Independence AND comprehend their doctrine and governing principles and agree that rights come with responsibilities – that America is a land of opportunity, not entitlement!

There is a huge difference between a citizen and a resident. Residents have a renter's mentality and a tourist's mindset. They often come for themselves and take all they can until it runs out. No one renting a car ever washes it, changes the oil, or rotates the tires! On 9/11 nineteen 'residents' who were living in our neighborhoods, shopping in our stores and taking flying lessons from our schools, attacked America.

In contrast, Citizens have an owner's mentality and clean, maintain and baby their vehicles and build for the future by giving more than they take so that resources never run out! A citizen knows that you never burn a bridge because you never know how many times you are going to have to cross it. Citizens don't say, 'America – love it or leave it.' We say 'America – keep it strong and committed to the principles on which it was founded or lose it!'

TWELVE BASIC UNIVERSAL LAWS

Laws that are always in play regardless
of whether or not you participate

The Law of Gravity: In existence long before the apple conked Newton on the head.

The Law of Physics: An object at rest will stay at rest. An object in motion will stay in its same velocity of motion. Neither will change unless an external force acts upon it.

The Law of Polarity - Everything is on a continuum and has and opposite. We can suppress and transform undesirable thoughts by concentrating on the opposite pole. It is the law of mental vibrations.

The Law of Relativity: Your viewpoint or perception of any event determines the reality you experience. This can apply to how you physically see or experience an event, or it can apply to how you emotionally perceive an event. In whatever event you experience, you have the power to control how you will respond.

The Second Law of Thermodynamics: When a hot substance is amalgamated with a cold substance, it quickly mixes, blends, and morphs into the same compromised, shared temperature, neither above nor below the median, called warm.

The Law of Vibration and Resonance: When anything in our universe, whether seen or unseen, is broken down into its purest and most basic form, it consists of pure energy or light, which exists as a vibratory frequency or pattern. These various vibratory patterns or frequencies are determined and projected based on thoughts, beliefs, and emotions. The resulting projected frequency engages the Law of Attraction, ensuring that we harmonize with energies that vibrate or resonate at a similar harmonious vibratory frequency, which determines our physical results.

The Law of Rhythm - Everything vibrates and moves to certain rhythms. These rhythms establish seasons, cycles, stages of development, and patterns. Each cycle reflects the regularity of God's Universe. Masters know how to rise above negative parts of a cycle by never getting too excited or allowing negative things to penetrate their consciousness.

The Law of Attraction: Ensures that whatever energy is broadcast into the universe is joined by (or attracted to) energies that are of an equal or harmonious frequency, resonance, or vibration. We don't attract who we want – we attract who we are. We attract what we believe we deserve.

The Law of Intuition: Being humble, quiet, and still enough to feel our promptings and tune into our inner knowing and ability in a non-rational, nonlinear way. We know something but we don't know how we know it. Most call this our "gut reaction," a reaction proved by science. In a ten-year study on people listening to their intuitive feelings, psychologist and science journalist Daniel Goleman isolated a large class of neurotransmitters in the brain called peptides. These occur in the gut and then move up through the chest, around the heart, and to the brain.

The Law of the Harvest, referred to as the Law of Cause and Effect: Any action produces or returns a result or outcome in exact proportion to the act or because that initiated it. It is also referred to as sowing and reaping, in that physical, mental, spiritual, emotional, social, financial, and familial creation is deter-mined by the kind and quality of seed that is planted. Through its predictable operation you can become conscious and purposeful in what you project or plant, which will, in turn, deter-mine what you will receive or harvest in each area of your life.

The Law of Reciprocity: Intricately connected with all universal laws, creating an unfailing process that reciprocates, meaning to give and take mutually and return in equal kind. What goes around always comes around.

The Law of Progression: Plato taught that all knowledge is recollection, which means when you hear or read something profound and agree with it, you are not learning anything new. You are recalling something you already learned in a previous experience. This is why we human beings sense that we are born inherently hardwired for progress with a natural craving for knowledge and fulfillment—and why it is logical that whatever degree of intelligence and experience we achieve in this life will rise with us in the next.

CHAPTER FOURTEEN

THE TWELVE HIGHEST LAWS OF THE UNIVERSE

The perfect analogy to differentiate between Basic Universal Laws that allow us to become 'successful' and the Advanced Universal Laws that inspire us to be 'Significant' is found in the comparison contrast of a tomato plant and a mighty oak tree. This healthy, strong, productive tomato plant is the perfect metaphor to illustrate those who are striving to be successful. Although it came from a good seed, has strong roots, and has brought forth luscious fruit appreciated by many, because the roots are shallow, it can support only a short season of success. After harvest, the tomato plant withers and must be replaced with new plants the next growing season. Like a tomato plant, success has a shelf life, is fleeting, has a defined end, and focuses on what we do instead of who we are becoming.

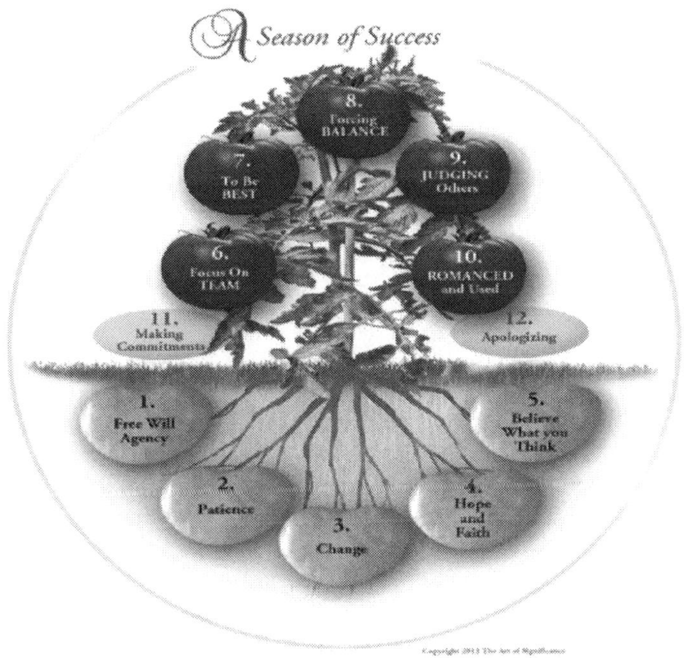

In contrast to the previous list of Basic Universal Laws and the rendition of the tomato plant with its short season of success, this depiction of an oak tree suggests a deep-rooted perennial Culture of Significance. Both the tomato plant and the oak tree begin with a tiny seed, but the acorn, when properly cultivated and nurtured, grows into something immovable and majestic with a life span of hundreds of years.

Though storm clouds may hover with high and restless winds, causing it to lose limb or two, because its roots are deep, the adversity only makes the mighty oak stronger as it continually stands unshakably solid, confidently firm, and appreciated by all. Unlike success, significance has no shelf life or final destination but is a continuous journey of growing, maturing, experiencing, persevering, and becoming everything we were born to be, that we may spread our branches to provide shade and assistance to any traveler who passes our way on a hot day.

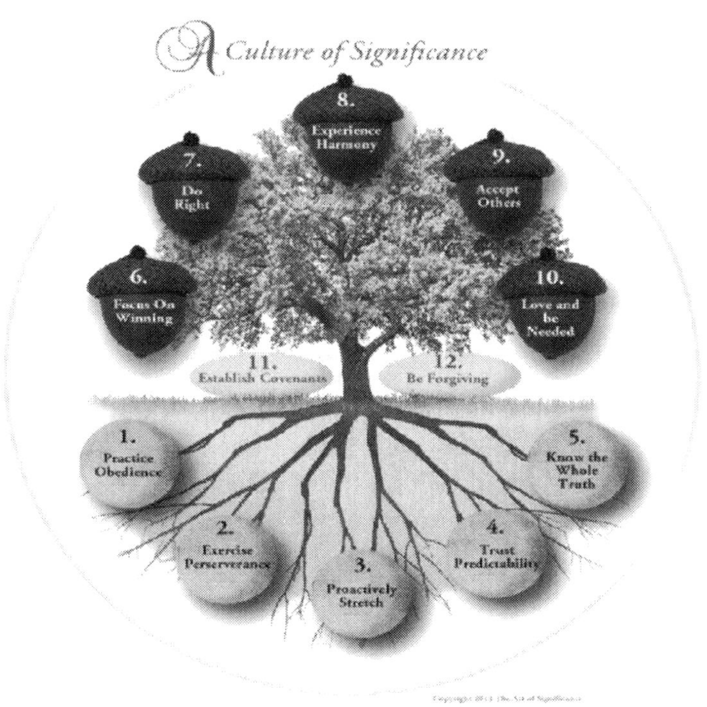

THE TWELVE HIGHEST UNIVERSAL LAWS
OF THE ART OF SIGNIFICANCE™

LAW 1: Practice Obedience Beyond Freewill Agency™

LAW 2: Exercise Perseverance Beyond Patience™

LAW 3: Proactively/Intentionally Stretch Beyond Change™

LAW 4: Trust Predictability Beyond Hope and Faith™

LAW 5: Know the Whole Truth Beyond What You Think™

LAW 6: Focus on Winning Beyond Team™

LAW 7: Do Right Beyond Seeking to Be the Best™

LAW 8: Experience Harmony Beyond Forcing Balance™

LAW 9: Accept Others Beyond Judging Them™

LAW 10: Love/Be Needed Beyond Romanced and Used

LAW 11: Establish Covenants Beyond Commitments™

LAW 12: Forgive Beyond Apologizing™

Obviously, these are the Advanced Universal Laws. The deepest comprehension of the Art of Significance is illuminated through the three-phase question and answer interactive experience we call A.R.T. When your Awareness grows and expands to the whole and complete truth about who you are—and you have a passionate inquisition into things as they really are—then you can and should focus on the Refinement of your identity, purpose, and beliefs, as well as on the actions that manifest those beliefs through continuous understanding.

This practice will immediately amalgamate into the Transformation process, which turns your success into significance through emotional application, and the never-ending cycle of A.R.T. continues. (Based On Dan's Bestselling Book, 'The Art Of Significance – Achieving The Level Beyond Success')

Practice Obedience over freewill agency. This is the ability to push beyond limits while exercising adherence to the boundaries of law. It also means respecting conscience, which is the highest possible law.

Exercise Perseverance beyond patience. Those who are patient and willing to wait for the time that "good things will come," are left in the dust by those who are persistently discontented in their efforts to perpetually go higher and achieve more.

Proactively Stretch instead of change. As an entrepreneur, many are content to push themselves to the point of being "impressive." But too few are willing to risk all to delve into a level that doesn't yet exist or is entirely unknown. Consider Uber. Or the Space X program being developed by Elon Musk. This trait is consistent among those who rise above success to significance.

Trust Predictability beyond hope and faith. Hope and faith, while they are admirable characteristics, pale quickly in comparison to the trust people and organizations can only gain by reliably delivering on their stated principles again and again. Think of the Mayo Clinic. Or Gandhi. Who are the five people you would trust if your life depended on it? Become one of those people for others. When you live up to your word as an unbreakable bond, you are not just successful, but you are significant as a leader, a family member, and as a friend.

Know The Whole Truth instead of believing what you think. Particularly in the aftermath of the recent election, we are seeing an avalanche of bias and bad will based on political alignments, ethnicity, gender, and even the personal opinions of those who report in the press. Learn to do deep research. In business, for example, if you are seeking a promotion, no matter how effective your current skills, what are the skills that are most required for the next step forward? Find out for yourself and learn them, rather than assuming that incompetence or discrimination is holding you back.

Focus On Winning instead of on team. In every contest, at least one team loses. In many markets, there are multiple losers. Team spirit, while valiant, is not a characteristic that leads to significance (nor in many cases to even success). Significance depends on standout individuals who are focused on winning perhaps not at all costs, but in principled ways, and are willing to motivate a team to the actions that ensure a winning objective is met.

Do Right instead of seeking to be best. Successful companies focus on being the best in their category. But "best" is only relevant next to what you compare it against. So what if you are the best video store? Remember Blockbuster? People who have the vision to determine what is right instead of best can take success to a new horizon--perhaps in safety, nutrition, or yes, even in delivering entertainment or education to a viewing audience.

Experience Harmony instead of forcing balance. As we attempt a work/life balance we juggle the balls of self, family, job and belief. But instead of juggling (which is certainly better than multitasking), strive to find harmonic balance, by being fully present and nourished by every note with no more and no less than its ideal emphasis within an integrated and harmonically beautiful whole. Learn to relish every note within the symphony that only you can create.

Accept Others instead of judging them. Instead of rushing to judgment, find the opportunity to listen to the stories of others. Attention is the highest form of motivation, psychologists say. Mentor instead of admonish. Write a note of appreciation to another individual, whether it be a family member, work associate, customer or partner each day.

Learn to Love and Be Needed instead of romanced and used. In a business sense, successful people are eager to "romance" and admire others based on selfish interests and a desire to use. But to love is a genuine and significant motive. My personal motto: "I like me best when I'm with you I want to see you again" speaks to the elements you should cultivate in yourself and align with and reward in others.

Establish Covenants beyond making commitments. "I'll get this done by tomorrow," or "Yes, I am with you," are shallow and meaningless when compared to covenants. Consider Winston Churchill offering up his "blood, sweat, toil and tears" to Great Britain "however long and hard the road may be" while Hitler's armies stormed Europe and Britain's ultimate fate was unknown. The ability to make and keep covenants is one of the greatest characteristics that sets Significant International Leaders apart.

Forgive instead of apologize. Perhaps the greatest characteristic of all is the ability to forgive unconditionally. Remember that through your lifetime, you, too, have spoken with insensitivity, have disappointed a loved one, and have made mistakes. You should amend these mistakes where you can. But even more importantly, you should forgive unconditionally the people who have offended you, regardless of their willingness to apologize or even to acknowledge their actions or guilt. This effort will attract a higher energy to your endeavors and will propel your results.

THE ART OF SIGNIFICANCE

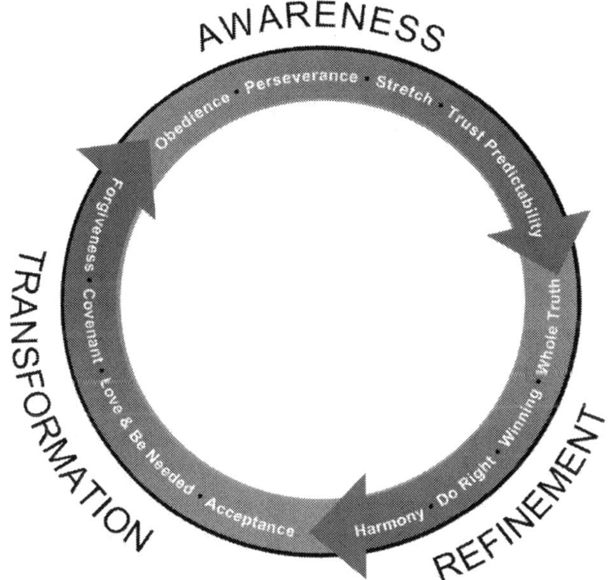

CHAPTER FIFTEEN

THE SIX 'RULES OF ENGAGEMENT'

IMPLEMENTING THE LAWS OF SIGNIFICANCE

"A bird sitting in a tree does not find her confidence in the strength of the branch, but in the strength of her own wings and ability to fly."

1. SCRATCH WHERE IT ITCHES

In medicine we know that prescription before diagnosis is malpractice. Thus, we have been conditioned to believe that to get a better answer we must ask a better question. True. But sometimes we need to question the answers. Sometimes we need to question the diagnosis, which could reveal a different prescription that finally leads to a cure. Too often we treat the symptom instead of the true cause of our pain.

A classic example of this is showcased every time we injure our bodies. If we twist and snap something in our knee and don't immediately go to a doctor to help us fix what is broken, because we are limping, it throws our back out of alignment and our back starts to hurt. After a while our back is so painful that we finally go to a spine specialist. But because it is our knee that is injured, and he is not aware of this, he can find nothing wrong with our back, and therefore, misdiagnoses our condition and only gives us medication to mask the pain. Hmm.

Doctors call this, "referred pain" where our discomfort is manifested somewhere in our body other than its real source. When it comes to getting and staying physically healthy and well we must always fix what is really broken.

If I was to ask you what is broken in your life, what would you tell me? And if I asked you what you were doing to fix it, what would you explain? Have your troubles and challenges been misdiagnosed? Misdiagnosis is happening everywhere.

To substantiate this, national statistics indicate that the K-12 school-based cases of ADD and ADHD (Attention Disorder) have risen 66% since 2005. ADD and ADHD are frontal lobe brain disorders, which is the part of the brain that plays a key role in higher mental functions such as motivation and social behavior. Are you telling me that out of nowhere, 66% of our youth have a frontal lobe problem? Where did that come from?

Irresponsible Misdiagnosis

This medical prognosis is a gross malpractice misdiagnosis that we should definitely discuss on another day. But FYI – Albert Einstein, Thomas Edison, Charles Lindberg, Henry Ford, John D. Rockefeller, Andrew Carnegie, Steven Jobs, Bill Gates, and Sir Richard Branson all share the misdiagnosis of ADHD.

In my home state of Utah our doctors prescribe 400% more Prozac for depression than doctors prescribe in any other state in the U.S. Are you kidding me? Utah has spectacular mountains to climb, rivers to fish, trails to hike, national parks to visit, and amazing and friendly, family focused residents who seek education and give service before self. There is no way that we have 400% more depressed people in Utah than in any other state! This is blatant and irresponsible misdiagnosis!!

The good news is that if your body breaks, when you go to the right doctor and he gives you the correct diagnoses, and he performs the necessary surgery or non-surgical procedures to stimulate your body to start healing itself, when you go through the proper steps of rehabilitation, the broken part of your body becomes stronger and more stable than it was before you injured it.

The same thing holds true for our attitudes, behaviors, broken hearts, shattered dreams, and how our life is turning out. If you think your life is in shambles and nothing like you want it to be, all you need to do is itemize what specific thing or things are broken, and find the right attitude doctor and behavioral specialist who can give you the correct diagnoses and rehabilitation plan, and help you help yourself 'scratch where it itches.'

2. SET YOUR THERMOSTAT

A thermostat is an instrument that focuses on inside conditions, measuring changes in circumstances that allow us to accurately predict and expect what the temperature will be. A thermostat is a component of an HVAC (heating and air conditioning) control sys-tem that senses the difference between actual temperature and de-sired set-point temperature. It switches heating and cooling devices on and off to maintain a desired temperature.

The moment you set the thermostat, it triggers a heater or air conditioner to run at full capacity until the set-point temperature is reached. Then it shuts off the equipment until it's needed again. In terms of our human set point, it is always dialed into the level of our self-esteem, sense of self-worth, and degree of personal development.

For example, how many times have we seen someone win 100 million dollars in the lottery only to be flat broke three years later? How many people do we know who go on a crazy diet and lose fifty pounds or more, but six months later they have gained all the weight back and more. Why is this?

It is simply because of their personal thermostat. No matter what happens on the outside with money, weight, relationships, promotions of authority, and so forth, ultimately our thermostat is going to kick in to bring our outside world to match our internal set point. In order to accumulate more in the outside world, the key to this equation is to become more on the inside.

In terms of personal and professional performance, behavior is driven by two kinds of expectations: Internal and External. Internal expectations are set for us by us and usually seek instant gratification. External expectations are set by others and usually seek long-term results. Our ability to delay gratification is a master skill, a triumph of the reasoning brain over the impulsive brain, a sign of emotional intelligence and stability that comes by being held accountable to high expectations.

3. RESETTING THERMOSTATS

As leaders, one of the most significant formulas for teaching others to reset their 'Thermostats' and set higher 'expectations' comes from the field of Special Education, where these amazing educators (like my daughter and master teacher Nikola) use a three-step evaluation process called the A-B-C Observation Sequence, sometimes referred to as S-R-S, or the Stimulus-Response-Stimulus.

- The "A" stands for the Antecedents, or what triggers the behavior.

- The "B" stands for the actual Behavior that results from the "triggers," or the antecedents.

- The "C" stands for the Consequences of the behavior.

In order to change someone's unwanted disobedient behavior to desired obedient behavior you have to figure out the motivation of their behavior, which could be one of these three things:

- To gain attention or something tangible
- To avoid or escape
- To receive sensory stimulation.

By determining the function of the behavior, you can then select a "target replacement behavior" that serves the same function and an intervention plan that will allow the child to turn inappropriate behaviors into appropriate behaviors – which obviously also applies to the corporate, military, government, athletic team and organizational responsibilities of a Leader, AND especially to managing, governing and changing the behaviors in ourselves!

4. FACE THE BRUTAL FACTS OF REALITY

Because some things are true whether we believe them or not; because everybody is entitled to an opinion but nobody is entitled to the wrong facts; and because we shouldn't believe everything that we think, it is crucial that we uncover, identify, quantify and itemize the true Facts about everything in the universe – beginning with our selves. Only then can we face the reality they present and figure out what to do about it if we don't like what we discover. And yes, the things we hate to hear the most are usually the things we need to hear the most!

A Life and Death Example of this was illuminated by America's POW- Prisoners of War during the Vietnam War. According to James Stockdale, a United States Navy vice admiral and aviator who was shot down in 1965 and held captive and inhumanely tortured for over seven years in the infamous 'Hanoi Hilton' Hoa Lo Prison, there was a distinct difference in the mindset of those POW's who survived and lived and those POW's who gave up and died before their release.

When asked about his coping strategy, Commander Stockdale, who was awarded the Congressional Medal of Honor for his gallantry and leadership as an incarcerated officer explained, "I never doubted that I would prevail in the end and turn the experience into the defining event of my life, which, in retrospect, I would not trade."

When asked who didn't make it out of the Vietnam prison, Stockdale replied: "It was the unrealistic optimists who said, 'We're going to be out by Christmas.' And Christmas would come, and Christmas would go. Then they'd say, 'We're going to be out by Easter.' And Easter would come, and Easter would go. And then

Thanksgiving, and then it would be Christmas again. And they died of a broken heart."

Those of us who lived and thrived confronted the most brutal Facts of our current reality, and never let our minds wander into the wish, would, may, might, should fictional world of what we could not control. Instead, we disciplined our selves to focus only on what we could control, which was the Fact that you had to deal with the pain – right now - of having your joints dislocated and limbs broken – so you could survive just in that moment to live just today, and return with honor to your prison cell to strengthen in any way possible, so you would live another day, knowing that one day at a time you could eventually return with honor to America!

Our Brutal Facts of Reality: In our everyday civilian world, everything Commander Stockdale observed in a military prison holds true for us in every way. In every situation we too must separate the Facts from our fictitious wishes and separate our brutal realities from our opinions and excuses and rationalizations for why these Facts exist.

For example, if the Facts show that you are physically weak, overweight and unhealthy, the unadulterated facts are: you ARE physically weak, overweight and unhealthy. Attaching your opinion and excuse for why you are in this miserable state doesn't change anything. "I don't have time to exercise" or "I need a Cola/Cookie sugar fix in the middle of the day" are actual causes of obesity! And, it is totally unacceptable to throw in the distorted rationalization that "at least I'm not as fat and sluggish as Joe or Jill."

The Guaranteed Solution: The body you want, the marriage you want, the family time you want, the spirituality you want, the bank account you want, the unlimited active lifestyle you want, the long and prosperous significant life you deserve, and the proof that what matters most is what lasts the longest, all start with the Facts!

5. "CHANGE OR DIE"

In the amazing and provocative book "Change or Die" author Alan Deutschman illuminates the research fact that 9 out of 10 people will not change their lifestyles and behaviors - even when their lives depend upon it. He asks, "What if you were given the choice – change or die - your own life or death for real? What if a trusted authority told you to make difficult and enduring changes in the way you think and act? If you didn't, your time would end soon — a lot sooner than it had to. Could you change when change really mattered? Yes, you say? Statistics prove otherwise.

An alarming example of this is found in the world healthcare crisis, an industry that consumes an astonishing $1.8 trillion a year in the United States alone, where 80% of the healthcare budget is consumed by a small minority of individuals with diseases that are very well known and behavioral. That is, they're sick because of how they choose to live their lives, not because of environmental, germ/viruses or genetic factors beyond their control, but because of smoking, drinking, eating, stress and not enough exercise – all preventable if they would only change!

Research shows that even patients with heart disease so severe that they undergo angioplasty stint procedures or coronary artery bypass surgery, refuse to change! Why? 90% of these patients revert back to their previous lifestyle within two years after surgery. Even though they know they have a serious heart condition and they know they should change their habits, they don't. No it's not they can't, it's they won't!"

Change Feelings: Conventional wisdom says that crisis is a powerful motivator for change, but it's not. Behavior change happens mostly by speaking to people's feelings. In highly successful change efforts, people help others see the Facts in ways that influence emotions, not just thought. The most critical challenge for businesses trying to compete in our turbulent world is not strategy, structure or systems. It's about changing the behavior of people.

Ironically, research from the Preventative Medicine Research Institute in Sausalito, California addresses this business reality in the context of healthcare stating, "Providing health information is important but we need to bring in the psychological, emotional, and spiritual dimensions that are so often ignored. Doctors have been trying to motivate patients mainly with factual analysis and the fear of death, and that simply isn't working. Fear may work, but only for a brief time. And people are frequently in denial and can't handle the facts, even when they confront them and clearly understand them.

For a few weeks after a heart attack, patients are scared enough to do whatever their doctors tell them. But death is just too frightening to think about, so their denial re-engages the coping strategies they've always used to deal with emotional troubles. Telling people who are lonely and depressed that they're going to live longer if they quit smoking, exercise, and change their diet is not that motivating. Who wants to live longer when you're in chronic emotional pain?"

So instead of frivolously trying to motivate patients with the "fear of dying," we simply rekindle in them the "joy of living" - convincing them they can feel better, not just live longer. Which means enjoying the things that make daily life pleasurable, like making love and spending quality time with loved ones and friends and taking long walks and golfing and skiing without the pain caused by their disease. Joy is a more powerful motivator than facts and fear! Love and camaraderie and service and feeling you are wanted, important and needed are more powerful motivators than facts and fear!

Solution Elements: In order for you to change yourself and inspire others to follow suit, you must be purposeful in your approach, your attitude, and your activities by focusing on seven key elements:

- Identify where you are right now in every aspect of your life. Remember: if you lie about your current location the directions to take you to where you want to go won't work!
- Get a clear understanding of the facts regarding what you must change
- Deepen your conviction and unshakeable belief on the reasons you will change

- Acquire the specific training, tools and techniques required to actually make the change
- Maintain a strong and consistent everyday work ethic that creates repeated experiences and short-term wins that sustain the change
- Leverage the power of community, basking in the knowledge, wisdom and experience of trusted mentors who will hold you accountable until you achieve the change
- Acknowledge the joy and enduring happiness that you will feel and experience as you subscribe to the Twelve Highest Universal Laws of Life Changing Leadership briefly listed in the previous Chapter Thirteen and fully illuminated in my Penguin Published book The Art of Significance.

6. USE "PLAY SLEEVE" EXECUTION TO CHOOSE LAWS

In the American sport of football, a National Football League Quarterback wears what is called a "Play Sleeve" on his forearm, which serves as a "Wrist Coach" that contains the names and symbols of the key plays in the team playbook.

The coach is on the sideline with his fingertips on the Facts called a 'Scouting Report' of the competition, coupled with an amalgamated strategic game plan that reveals the best play options they should use to solve the ever-changing challenges at hand.

This allows the coach and his quarterback to know the real time Facts and decide and communicate in real time, which play should be called in each specific and new situation to most effectively and efficiently deal with the Facts and get the job done.

* Intangible Fact: If the coach and the quarterback have not previously 'Set' their personal 'Thermostats' to a high self-esteem, high confidence level based on their preparation, which includes knowing who they are and the personal power they possess to deal with the Facts presented by the opposing team and the ever changing circumstances on the field, then all the 'Play' calling and use of the 'Play Sleeve/Wrist Coach' will go for not!

In this mindset, you need to now think of the Twelve Highest Universal Laws of the Art of Significance as the metaphorical list of your twelve key plays that constitute your playbook. As you learn and study and master these laws to the point they become automatic thoughts and action step behaviors, they become your "Play Sleeve" that you constantly wear day and night, at home, at work, at play, that you can use in real time to solve every challenge that comes your way.

Regardless of the personal or professional dilemma or brutal Facts of your current reality, because you have mastered the Art of Significance and fully comprehend each law, you need only face the situation, listen to garner all of the available information, and then pause to check your "Play Sleeve" list of plays (in your mind or in your downloaded study guide training manual that you carry in your briefcase) and decide which of the twelve laws, or which combination of the laws will help you have your crucial conversation and effectively turn the problem into a challenge that you can actually solve or begin to solve in that moment.

CHAPTER SIXTEEN

SIGNIFICANT PARTNERS ATTRACT SIGNIFICANT PARTNERS

"Depth of friendship does not depend on length of acquaintance. *It's Not Who You Know – It's Who Knows You."*

In a chain of "significant connections" where and when and how will you emerge? Because we become the average of the five people we associate with the most, we must be willing to pay any price and travel any distance to associate with extraordinary significant human beings. Because I have met many of the most extraordinary people on the planet, I am often asked by my colleagues to introduce them to the likes of Michael Jordan, Brad Paisley, and Sir Richard Branson.

"Learn to kite surf," I tell them, "find out where Branson kite surfs, and I'm certain you'll run across him on the water, beach and/or parking lot as you are gathering your gear or putting it away for the day. Because you share a similar passion for the same sport, and only 1% of the world is part of your tiny fraternity, most likely Branson will initiate a conversation, which may lead to an invitation to join Sir Richard and his surfing buddies for cocktails and dinner. And if you are articulate, unpretentious, with manners and a sense of style, you will be asked about yourself, your family, your job, your ambitious dreams, and who knows what? Maybe even to keep in touch when the evening comes to an end."

Remember, the DNA of a serial entrepreneur like Sir Richard Branson sustains a natural curiosity about products, processes, places and people and how to make them better – which includes asking you what you do, why you do it, and especially how can he help you do it better by introducing you to friends, potential customers and investors?

Get involved at the highest levels of motorcycle racing and you'll interact with Michael Jordan and his Jordan Motorsport team at every race. Become an extraordinary fly fisherman and you can invite Paisley and his celebrity friends on a weekend adventure.

PLACE OF ENTRY

The point here is not about meeting Branson, Jordan and Paisley. The point is to understand the Place of Entry to engage in a meaningful way with Branson, Jordan, Paisley and all of the superstars of the 1% crowd who constitute the very small community who have the income and time to get involved in humanitarian causes, with the ability to travel and control their schedule in the pursuit of extreme recreation. This eliminates 99% of the population, and through statistical probability, it is easier to track down 1% of the population than 99%. When it comes to connecting with the influential and associating with the high net worth 'movers and shakers,' these superstars are so busy becoming successful, that they don't have time to be introduced to you in their offices!

The place to meet the top 1% is to go where they are significantly engaged in their passionate hobbies, recreational loves, appreciation of the performing arts, favorite sporting events, and charitable fundraising galas. For it is in these exhilarating meaningful environments that you connect at the heart and soul, emotional feeling level, which is always a prerequisite to connecting at the intellectual financial level.

ENTERING HIGHER LEVELS OF LEADERSHIP

When it comes to the "Place of Entry" in leadership, advancing in one's career and climbing the corporate ladder may well be in your future, but only when you first connect with the people who create these growth opportunities. Income and making more money is just a byproduct of your relationship with influential people. Impress the boss and you get the pay raise. You will never receive a promotion unless the individual above you in the leadership/management 'food chain' agrees to it.

Your ability to move from one level of leadership up to the Place of Entry of the next level of leadership is dependent upon your desire and effort to connect and bond with someone who has a title, authority and responsibility at the level above your current standing. We call these influencers "sponsors" who are trusted enough by their peers to invite you to their social functions and recommend you for greater company involvement. In the previous example of Sir Richard Branson, you gained access to him by engaging in the same activity for the same reasons, and created trust during cocktails and dinner until he felt comfortable in 'sponsoring' you into his inner circle of influential leaders.

SPONSORED?

How does one find and choose such a "sponsor?" You don't. You can't. He/she must choose you! How, where, when, why? Simply, the Place of Entry in leadership is only created when you avoid a clash of cultures by engaging in the same attitude, values, expectations, conversation, wardrobe, and recreation of those at the next highest level of leadership. The blatant example of this is illustrated in the 1960's television series, 'The Beverly Hillbillies,' where this uneducated, unsophisticated 'hick family from the sticks' struck oil on their farm in the back woods of West Virginia, and with their sudden wealth moved to Beverly Hills, California into a mansion and glamorous world of fame and sophisticated elegance.

But because they continued to speak with poor grammar, calling their swimming pool a 'cement pond' and continued to wear their bib overalls, dirty boots and out of fashion homemade dresses, they were never invited into the inner circle of influence, which would have created 'upward mobility' in their neighborhood, community and leadership opportunities to serve.

SERV:
SELF. EXECUTION. REPUTATION. VISIBILITY

For this reason, I have identified four elements in the formula for moving up in any organization and profession and advancing from one level of leadership to the next. I call it: S.E.R.V. – Self, Execution, Reputation, Visibility. You must honestly acknowledge your weaknesses, limitations, strengths and purpose and commit to bettering your Self. You must consistently Execute at the highest level. You must cultivate the right Reputation. And, you must manage your Visibility so the right people will know you, witness your character and experience your extraordinary Execution.

Each of the four S.E.R.V. elements are woven into every job description, every career advancement opportunity, every pay raise and every new leadership responsibility and carries a different weight in upward mobility:

SELF is 40% of the Place of Entry and is based on your understanding that the definition of sales is 'the transference of trust' and we love to do business with winners. For this reason, you don't attract who you want – you attract who you are – you attract what you believe you deserve in an intimate relationship with a spouse or significant other, in a friendship, in your teammates, in your place of employment, in a job description and leadership responsibilities, in a neighborhood, in the car you drive, in the toys you own, in the holidays you take, and in your desire to concentrate on perfecting your Execution.

Obviously, in order to attract high class, character and integrity based, extraordinary people into your life you must first BE a high class, character and integrity based, extraordinary person, so leaders and coworkers choose you, not just somebody who does what you do! So the questions are: what makes you who you are? What can you change and what can you not change that makes you more attractive?

What parts of you are transferable from relationship to relationship, from job to job and from location to location?

WHAT'S TRANSFERABLE AND NOT TRANSFERABLE

We have all attended classes over the years where instructors teach that because we all have unlimited potential, if we will just attend the right seminars, we will be able to change and become everything that our leaders and managers want us to be.

This is absurd. Some things are teachable, learned, and transferable, but others are inherent and un-trainable. For this reason, we must never heap all things into the same seminar pile by remembering the differences between Knowledge, Skill, and Talent, and comprehending how they interface one with another.

KNOWLEDGE is simply what you are aware of. There are two kinds of knowledge: Factual Knowledge is what you know; Experiential Knowledge is what understanding you have picked up along the way. Knowledge can be taught and learned and transferred to others. However, it is usually situational and specific, working hand in hand with the acquired skills you learned in training. Knowledge is power, but it has no heart. Reason leads to conclusions but it is emotion that leads to action.

You can have understanding without knowledge, but having knowledge without understanding is worthless. We don't learn to know; we learn to do. Understanding our knowledge is the why to taking action. Although we will always retain our knowledge and wisdom in this life and throughout eternity, most likely the specific education and information required for one specific job is not transferable to a different job, which requires that we be life-long learners.

SKILLS are the how-to, practical application of the what. Like knowledge, skills are capabilities that can be taught and learned and transferred from one person to another. Skills are specific and situational, and they are acquired. Most likely, one specific specialty skill set is not transferable to a different job, which means that we continuously seek the latest training.

TALENT is commonplace. There is nothing special about talent. Everybody is born with specific reoccurring patterns of thought, feeling, and behavior, all of which constitute what we call talents. Our natural abilities to play music or paint or dance or play a specific sport or excel at math are God given talents that we can either work on and strengthen or neglect. They are a part of us because of a genetic class of chromosomes passed on to us by our parents.

At one end of the spectrum we have Mozart, the prolific composer of the classical era who showed prodigious ability from his earliest childhood. Obviously he was born with an extraordinary musical talent already manifested by the age of five when he was competent on keyboard and violin and performed before European royalty. At 17, Mozart was engaged as a musician at the Salzburg court, but then returned to Vienna where he composed most of his best-known symphonies, concertos, and operas, and portions of the Requiem, until his early death at the age of 35.

On the other end of the spectrum we have the naturally gifted, fast running, high jumping talented athlete who was born with exceptional speed, strength, agility and eye-hand coordination. And although he could be the very best in the world if he would simply work hard and compete against himself, he takes his talent for granted and remains content to only be better than those he is competing against today. Most likely the specific talent required to do one specific job is not the same talent required to do a different job, which means we must constantly strengthen our natural talents and keep them finely tuned for whatever opportunities present themselves.

For all of these reasons, the only thing that is transferable from relationship to relationship, from job to job and from location to location is our attitude toward fully developing our Knowledge, Skills and Talents, which constitute the whole and complete 'Self.'

WHAT'S HOLDING YOU BACK?

For over thirty years I have reminded people of two fundamental truths: "When your attitude is right your abilities will always catch up." "No matter what your past has been you have a spotless future." Do you believe it? Research shows that we spend 80 percent of our waking hours with our minds focusing on and drifting into either the past or the future.

The past isn't just a year ago or a week ago – it's twenty minutes ago. It's thinking 'I can't believe she said that to me, it really hurt my feelings.' It's thinking 'my son was angry when he left last night and I need to repair the damage.' In golf, it's thinking about the putts you missed that caused your double-bogey and dwelling on it until you get the 'yips' and can't concentrate on making the next putts that would win the tournament. It's thinking 'How dare the company downsize me and let me go when I was the most senior employee,' when in reality you had never upgraded your training and expanded your skillset to remain irreplaceable! This is living in the past.

We think of the future as being next week, next month or next year. But in reality it's twenty minutes from now. It's thinking 'I wonder what's for lunch? Thinking 'what should I wear to dinner?' Thinking 'I wonder what she will think of me if I do this?' Thinking 'what if I fail?' so you don't even try. Thinking 'what if my teenager gets kidnapped?' so you never let her travel with friends. Thinking 'what if I work harder than anyone and no one notices?' so you never give it your all.

All regret, sadness, anger and bitterness come when our mind is focused on the past. All stress, anxiety, worry and fear enter our mind when we are thinking about the future. In both mindsets we are frozen in our ability to focus on the present – and only in the present can we learn from the past so we can turn our future into reality!

* Alert! Self is not only a Place of Entry, but oftentimes it is also the Place of Closure, where you decide to stop pursuing upward mobility because it requires that you leave a certain set of friends behind, and this is too high a price to pay.

I've seen this in a company that employs 'Organized Labor' where a standout employee is offered a promotion to a leadership role on the management side. But because his brothers in the Labor

Union accuse him of 'selling out' he turns down the opportunity to climb the corporate ladder. The tragedy in this is that it has nothing to do with compromising his values or turning his back on his friends. It has to do with what each of us have already experienced or what you will yet encounter at your ten-year high school class reunion.

CLASS REUNION

We all show up and immediately connect with old friends and interact with acquaintances we wish we had gotten to know. For the first 90 minutes we reminisce and laugh about the old boyfriend/girlfriend relationships that didn't end up in marriage, with someone singing Garth Brook's song, "Thank God For Unanswered Prayers." We engage in small talk about teachers, rivalry games, fights, dances and the time Johnny snuck a donkey in through the back door and let it loose in grouchy Ms. Crotchet's library. But then something happens.

We start running out of things to talk about and naturally start to gather in new and different groups with people whose lives are currently in line with ours. Those who are still single and 'party animals' looking for a wild and crazy time connect at that level. Those who are stuck in their past, still living in the 'glory days' when 'Uncle Rico' threw the touchdown pass that won the game, are connecting at that level. Those who are married with children are connecting at that level. Those who have started businesses or who have become rich and famous are connecting at that level.

Just as we formed 'Clicks' in high school based on our likes and dislikes, sports, music, arts, hobbies and health habits, in less than two hours at our reunion we have done the same thing. No, we did not suddenly feel we were better than our old friends. Because of certain decisions that everybody at the reunion had made, everyone had progressed in different directions at different speeds. And some had not progressed at all.

When it comes to the Place of Entry, one's Self esteem and Self-development will determine the friends and associates we attract, which in turn will influence the decisions we make and whether or not we choose to let go of the past and accept opportunities to become the very best version of our Self.

COMPLACENT OR MOTIVATED?

Out of my own curiosity about the differences between high achievers and those content to remain average, I decided to conduct my own visual survey. As unscientific as it is, I took my idea aboard the planes I flew in for a calendar year and discovered something very intriguing. I have been blessed to fly first class on most of my 6 million miles on Delta Airlines, and on each of the 120 round trip flights that I flew in a twelve month period, I walked to the rear of the plane, turned around and made my way through 'coach' back to the front until I returned to my seat 2A.

Do you know what I discovered? The people sitting in 'coach' who had purchased a low cost ticket, forcing them to eat pathetic food, squished into the person sitting next to them, were watching a movie, playing video games or sleeping. In contrast, everyone in first class who had purchased a different experience with more room, better food, unlimited drinks and snacks, was working on his/her computer, reading, writing or listening to a podcast/speech. No one was sleeping or watching TV. They had turned their travel time into self-development, educational time – a university in the sky, validating the incredible insight of my mentor and friend Jim Rohn:

"Life responds to deserve and not to need.
It doesn't say, 'If you need, you will reap.'
It says, 'If you plant, you will reap.'
Poor people have big TVs.
Rich people have big libraries!"

With all do respect and no judgment intended, apparently those flying in coach were followers, caught in a minimum requirement mediocre complacency, content with their personal and professional results. However, those in first class were apparently leaders, caught in a maximum opportunity to better them selves.

It's true. In sports, in business, in the military, as a spouse and significant other, as a parent, coworker, neighbor, friend, the difference between a successful/significant person and an unsuccessful person is that the successful/significant person will do what the unsuccessful person will not do. The successful/significant person doesn't want to do it either, but he/she does it any way!

Bottom line. Becoming the very best version of your Self attracts the attention of extraordinary coaches who 'recruit' you to play on their championship teams. Think about this before you continue and decide who you are and what you will do about your Self!

CHAPTER SEVENTEEN

BECOMING A SIGNIFICANT PARTNER WHO ATTRACTS SIGNIFICANT PARTNERS

(CONTINUATION)

SELF. EXECUTION. REPUTATION. VISIBILITY

EXECUTION is only 10% of the Place of Entry. Shocking I know, but it's because Execution and doing the job you are paid to do is really only 'making the team' and practicing so you get in the game. The people with whom you work are good at Execution or they would not have been hired and would have been fired! Perfecting your Execution and becoming a peak performer, only lands you a 'starting position,' which results in more playing time. Most organizations have a merit pay system that clearly demonstrates that the better the Execution and higher the productivity, the more money a person can earn. The stars on the team enjoy the fame and fortune, but only because they understand if they are not training and pushing themselves to their ultimate capacity and potential as human beings, someone else, somewhere else, is. And when they meet them, they will win!

Alert! In the midst of improving your performance and perfecting your Execution, you must remember that the skills used in your current job are usually not the same skills needed at the next level. Great players don't necessarily make great coaches. Great sales professionals don't necessarily make great sales managers. For this reason, although organizations pay for Execution and peak performance, they definitely promote based on potential. This is why Execution is only 10% of the Place of Entry.

Bottom line. Great Execution gets you on the field and playing the game. Perfected Execution lands you a starting position, more playing time and a chance to become a star in your league.

REPUTATION is 20% of the Place of Entry and is cultivated in two different, yet overlapping dimensions: Inside Rep and Outside Rep. Your Outside Reputation is constantly on display at home, at work, and at play, as a visible expression of how you feel about yourself, where you are physically, mentally, spiritually, emotionally, socially and financially in your life and where you yearn to go. The way you walk, the way you sit, the clothes you wear and your language (good grammar/poor grammar, please/thank you, foul mouth/sophisticated elegance, social graces, etc.) send a strong message to your fellow coworkers and organizational leaders that "I'm ready" or "I'm not ready" to fit into the leadership culture of excellence and play the game at the next level.

In fact, it is critical for you to become 'fluent' in the language of the next level of leadership before you are officially invited to join. For it is this 'Fluency' that gives you the ability to communicate and fit into an environment without conscious thought and instantaneously become one of the boys or girls!

Your Inside Reputation is cultivated when you commit to 'walking on higher ground' and holding yourself accountable to an extraordinary set of expectations. As a boy I was a proud member of Troop 595 in the Boy Scouts of America, where I participated in character building experiences and learned core values that shaped my life forever. There is no better list of governing principles from which to regulate our thoughts and actions than the twelve itemized in the 'Scout Law,' where we all should commit to being:

Trustworthy and always telling the truth, keeping every promise; Loyal to those who are not present – refusing to gossip and always defending irrefutable truths; Helpful and willingly doing things for others without pay or reward; Friendly to all, because there is strength in diversity; Courteous and polite to everyone, regardless of age or position; Kind knowing there is strength in being gentle and treating others as we want to be treated; Obedient in following the 'family rules' and obeying the laws of community and country; Cheerful and positively approaching everyday with gratitude while striving to make others happy; Thrifty by carefully using time, protecting and conserving natural resources and saving for a 'rainy day'; Brave and courageous to stand for what is right even if others laugh at or threaten; Clean and keeping body and mind fit and pure, and home and community spotless; Reverent toward the sacred sanctity of life, acknowledging God, respecting the beliefs of others.

When you are living by these twelve governing 'Inside' principles, the cultivation of your Outside Reputation becomes important, clear, constant and simple (not necessarily easy) and gets the attention of future 'sponsors' who believe you should be given more responsibility at work with an accompanying leadership promotion in the organization!

Bottom line. Cultivating your Inside Reputation proves leadership is a not a noun, it's a verb - not appointed, but earned through respect. Cultivating your Outside Reputation proves that you don't just talk-the-talk, you walk-the-walk and are ready for additional responsibility and the accompanying promotion, which on a team means you are voted 'Captain.' You are now a member of an elite group of leaders in your league.

VISIBILITY is 30% of the Place of Entry and is the only way you will ever be invited to play out of your league – in a higher, more prestigious, bigger, faster, stronger league with premier players making maximum salaries. For this reason, it is critical to enhance and increase personal Visibility and meaningful exposure at every level of your organization. When the leaders have a position to fill, they will see your attitude, knowledge, skill and talent, and realize you are already fluent in upper level languages, which will ensure a smooth transition in this succession planning and make you the obvious choice for promotion.

Getting Visibility and meaningful exposure inside the organization includes volunteering for internal projects, asking for more responsibility within a specific job function, being willing to learn new skills and experience different assignments to broaden your understanding of the entire enterprise, and showing up early to work and staying late when necessary without expecting to be paid overtime.

Getting meaningful outside Visibility and exposure includes getting involved in the community, supporting local charities, volunteering to coach youth teams, joining Kiwanis, Lions, Optimists, Rotary, and chairing company sponsored activities.

Remember, when it comes to creating 'Upward Mobility' and networking your way to promotions, pay raises and greater influence at work, at play, and in the world, it's not about who you know – it's about who knows you are constantly striving to better your SELF, who knows you EXECUTE with perfection, who knows your REPUTATION is impeccable, and who knows you are VISIBLE using your leadership skills to support the things that matter most!

Bottom line. Significant Partner Leaders Attract Significant Partner Leaders because they Play Big and Live Bigger – 'Go Big or Go Home.' Marianne Williamson said it best:

"Our deepest fear is not that we are inadequate. Our deepest fear is that we are powerful beyond measure. It is our light, not our darkness that most frightens us. We ask ourselves, 'Who am I to be brilliant, gorgeous, talented, fabulous?' Actually, who are you not to be? You are a child of God. Your playing small does not serve the world. There is nothing enlightened about shrinking so that other people won't feel insecure around you. We are all meant to shine, as children do.

We were born to make manifest the glory of God that is within us. It's not just in some of us; it's in everyone. And as we let our own light shine, we unconsciously give other people permission to do the same. As we are liberated from our own fear, our presence automatically liberates others."

CHAPTER EIGHTEEN

LEADING SELF THROUGH 'STANDARD DEVIATIONS'

"The difference between being a champion who wins and an 'also ran' is small yet significant"

In baseball, having a .200 batting average means you hit safely on base two out of ten times up to bat. Obviously, to have a .300 batting average means you hit safely on base three out of ten times up to bat. The difference between a .200 hitter and a .300 hitter is only one hit in every ten times up to bat. Yet the .200 hitters make minimum salary and are traded from team to team as often as a manager changes his dirty socks. A .300 hitter makes maximum salary and is always a star and one of the league leaders. If the batters let the count go to full count – 3 balls, 2 strikes every time they are up to bat, then the difference between a .200 hitter and a .300 hitter is only one hit in every 60 pitches!

The difference between a champion and second place – between a leader and a follower, is simply a little bit of extra effort – that "some-thing more." Some call it the "IT" factor, as in, "That champion has it – that superstar's got it." When they walk into a room people stop and ask, "Who is he/she and what does he/she do?"

In the music business it's the difference between an artist and a singer – the difference between experiencing the performance of Celine Dion and listening to the winner of a karaoke competition. They both sing the same song and the same notes, but Celine allows the music to emotionally move her to perform in a higher dimension where she makes the song her own. And, the other singer just stays on pitch and sings it like everybody else.

Because we used baseball batting averages as our example of peak performance, let us also use numbers and statistics to showcase the differences between peak performance and mediocrity in every aspect of life – physical, mental, spiritual, emotional, social, financial, family, recreation and charitable giving. The following is a brief explanation of how each of our performances can be broken down from highest achievement to average achievement to no achievement. As you read and ponder this scientific formula, ask your self at what level are you currently performing?

STANDARD DEVIATIONS

In the framework of statistical analysis, this difference between being average and part of the norm, above average, successful, and achieving an extraordinary level of significance is measured in increments called "Standard Deviations."

From our college statistics classes we know that a Standard Deviation is a measurement of variability or diversity used in probability theory. It shows how much variation or dispersion there is from the average mean or expected value. A low standard deviation indicates that the data points tend to be very close to the mean, which is called the normal distribution of data, whereas high standard deviation indicates that the data is spread out over a large range of values.

Standard deviation is commonly used to measure confidence in statistical conclusions. For example, the margin of error in polling data is determined by calculating the expected standard deviation in the results if the same poll were to be conducted multiple times. In science, researchers commonly report the standard deviation of experimental data, and only the effects that fall far outside the range of standard deviation are considered statistically "significant." The standard deviation is the statistic that helps us find the story behind the data, which assigns a specific value to the results.

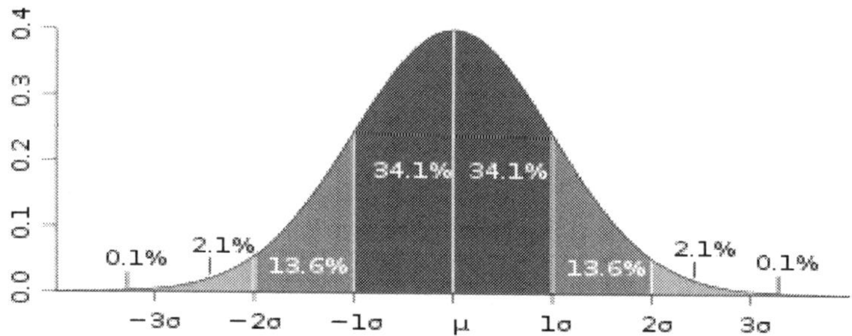

One Standard Deviation is calculated at 34.1 % in measuring both negative, lackadaisical performance, and positive improvement performance. Aggregately these individuals constitute 68.2% of the performers, i.e., the average norm, majority, mean or bulk of the sampled batch. These are the wannabe worker bees stuck in mediocrity, getting by with minimum requirement, who hate their short term jobs, who only look forward to Friday instead of Monday, who think they are paid by the hour, expect to find value and meaning at work, and say they are bored, which means they think it is their community's responsibility to entertain them, and their employer's responsibility to make their lives matter.

They won't come early or stay late unless you pay them overtime, they are lousy neighbors who barely groom their yard, never plant flowers, never shovel their driveway and sidewalks when it snows, whine that their glass is half empty, and feel entitled to rights without responsibility.

Two Standard Deviations engulf the individuals who are either 13.6% lazier and non-performing than the majority, or that much more driven and productive than the norm. On the positive side, these are they who are considered above average, who love their jobs as long term careers, who know they are paid for the value they bring to each hour, who realize that value is brought to and created at work, who know it's not the size of the town, but the size of the dream – not the size of the dog, but the size of the fight in the dog that determines it's success.

They become middle managers, are good neighbors with manicured yards and planted flowers, who always shovel their walks when it snows. They are recognized for excellence and receive high awards as outstanding employers and employees, and always have winning records as coaches and players. They know success is an opportunity not a guarantee, their glass is half full, and that freedom is about rights because of responsibility.

Three Standard Deviations categorize those, who on the negative side, have given up on love, life and the pursuit of happiness. On the positive side, these are the amazing 2.1% who are at the top of their game: Olympians, professional athletes, CEO's, CFO's, COO's, organizational presidents, military general officers and senior NCO's, outstanding physicians and nurses, incredible attorneys, engineers, sales professionals, and members of Million Dollar Round Table, local television anchormen and women, district school superintendents, exceptional school teachers, championship winning coaches, community activists, PTSA presidents, scoutmasters, and involved parents. Senators, congressmen, congresswomen, governors, mayors, astronauts, big time players who make big plays in big games, and yes, each of the thoroughbred horses who race in the Kentucky Derby also positively fall into this Third Deviation.

They are great neighbors whom you can count on in every positive and negative situation, who shovel the walks of the widows and the elderly when it snows, who challenge the fact that even though their glass is half full it better not be full of the wrong thing, and take responsibility to lead the fight for freedom.

Four Standard Deviations reveal the 0.1% who are far outside the bell curve range of results. On the far left side of the graph, these are those precious souls with significant disabilities and severe mental illness. Obviously it is this elite, extraordinary few in the positive right side analysis who are the focus of this book.

These are the social deviants who understand that in order to get traction you need friction; who are not trying to deliver "value-add," but rather impact! These are the day dreamers who use the night; the edgy yet respectful; visionary yet focused; eccentric yet disciplined; confident yet teachable; charismatic, driven, resourceful, peculiar and proud of it, whom we revere and honor because they have transformed themselves and their lives from successful to "Significant."

These are the greatest of the great – the inspiration to the inspirational, put in a class by themselves by incredible leaders such the extraordinary U.S. Presidents including George Washington, Thomas Jefferson, Abraham Lincoln, John F. Kennedy, and Ronald Reagan, extraordinary General Secretary of the U.S.S.R Mikhail Gorbachev, extraordinary patriot, revolutionary reformer and first President of Poland Lech Walesa, extraordinary British Prime Ministers Sir Winston Churchill and Margaret Thatcher, and the incredibly extraordinary, visionary leader and architect/founder/father of the United Arab Emirates: His Highness Sheikh Zayed bin Sultan Al Nahayan.

These top 0.1% are the Nobel Prize Laureates, Secretaries of State and Secretaries/Ministers of Defense, Speakers of the House, ambassadors, supreme court justices, world record holders, Olympic gold medalists, championship winning coaches, World Series, Super Bowl, NBA Finals and NCAA tournament MVP's, #1 ranked players in their individual sports, superstar CEO's of major corporations, world renown surgeons, architects and engineers, Military Four Star Generals, Command Chief Master Sergeants, Chairmen of the Joint Chiefs of Staff, Congressional Medal of Honor recipients, astronauts who walked on the moon, and national television network anchormen and women. As in horse racing, every horse that competes in the Kentucky Derby is a valuable thoroughbred stallion who has won races elsewhere, but only one of them wins the "roses" that day.

BEING 'FULLY ALIVE!'

Authority, power, fame or fortune never drives Motivation To Be In The Top 0.1% Fourth Deviation. Significant Partner Leaders know that the only way to truly inspire our colleagues and subordinates to motivate themselves to increase performance, is when we help them answer three critical questions in every task we are asking them to do:

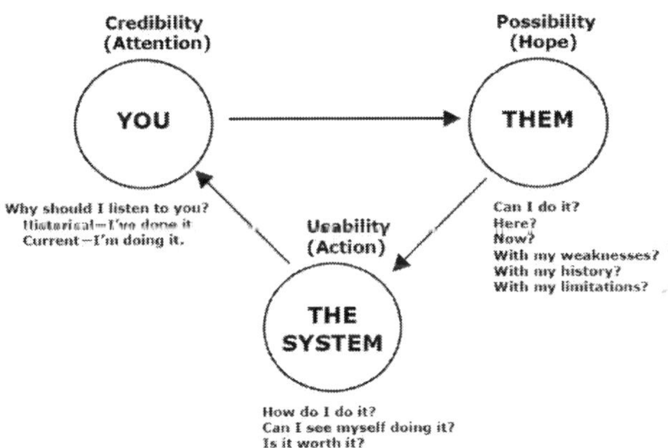

"Why Should I Listen To You?" (This is the Credibility piece - Have you done it? Are you currently doing it?)

"Can I Do It Too?" (This is the Hope piece - With my weak-nesses and limitations? With my strengths?)

"Where Do I Go From Here?" (This is the Action piece - How do I do it? What should I do next? Is it worth it to me?)

The quickest way for Significant Partner Leaders to answer these three questions is to "live like you're dying." Yeah, "you could have missed the pain, but then you'd have had to miss the dance." So, "when given the chance to sit it out or dance, I hope you'll dance!" J. Stone said it best:

The most visible creators are
those artists whose medium is life itself.
The ones who express the inexpressible
- without brush, hammer, clay or guitar.
They neither paint nor sculpt – their medium is being.
Whatever their presence touches increases life.
They see and don't have to draw.
They are the Artists of Being Alive!
J. Stone

CHAPTER NINETEEN

LEADING BY CORE VALUES

L.E.A.D.E.R.S.H.I.P.

LOYALTY

- Bear allegiance to something or someone significant. Believe in and devote yourself to your organization and stand up for your teammates.

EXCELLENCE IN ALL YOU DO

- Never settle for anything less than maximum effort. This goes for the physical, mental, spiritual and emotional sides of life.

ATTITUDE

- You can if you think you can. When your attitude is right, your abilities will always catch up.

DUTY

- Fulfill your obligations. Carry out your assigned missions, tasks and responsibilities - all in constant motion. Build one assignment onto another, until each one is completed.

ENGAGED

- Proactively, intentionally participate and stay involved. Prove to yourself that you are needed.

RESPECT

- Obey higher authority and follow moral/ethical ideals. Treat people as they want to be treated, expecting others to do the same.

SERVICE BEFORE SELF

- Put the welfare of others before your own. Do your duty loyally without thought of recognition or gain and go a little further, enduring a little longer. Look a little closer to see how you can add to the effort.

HONOR

- Live all of these ten Significant International Leadership values. Live them not be-cause others expect it, but because you demand it of yourself.

INTEGRITY

- Trustworthily do what's right, legal and moral. Do and say nothing that deceives others, beginning with the fundamental acceptance of your self.

PERSONAL COURAGE

- Face fear, danger or adversity (physical or moral). With physical courage, it is a matter of enduring physical duress and at times risking personal safety. With moral courage, it's continuing forward on the right path, especially if taking those actions is not popular with others.

Which is your strongest attribute? Why? Which value is your weakest that you need/want to strengthen?

CHAPTER TWENTY

LEADING BY ORIENTATION

Successful leaders and managers have a task-oriented style and focus on deadlines and production. When asked about their profession, they always emphasize the enterprise and what and how they do what they do. They are human "doings" who see the glass half full. But they still take no for an answer, because they accept minimum requirement with an outlet to deflect their lack of production onto others whenever they encounter a stumbling block. Their language is filled with blaming innuendos explaining "it's the economy," or "they don't know what they're talking about," or it's "their" fault or "yea, but...," Or "I can't" when they really mean "I won't," or the complacent non-energetic "I'm burned out."

Significant Partner Leaders and Managers have a relationship-oriented style and focus on why they are doing what they do, who they are doing it with and for, and how they can help others around them do it better. When asked about their profession, they always emphasize the greater purpose of their work and the difference they are making for the end user of their product and/or service. They are human "beings" who see the glass is half full, but realize it could be half full of the wrong thing. They continuously challenge the status quo because the sale doesn't begin until the customer says no. Their language is grounded in knowing there is always a way - they just need to uncover every option and alternative. They know that if for some reason they feel "burned out" it means that once upon a time they were lit, and it's not going to take much to rekindle their flame and get it burning again! They then use their fire-starter attitude and skills to re-fire others!

- Is your leadership/management language successful or significant?
- Do you **Preach?** "Do it because I said so."
- Do you **Teach?** "Do it because I do it."
- Do you **Reach?** "Go where others are physically and emotionally, and invite."
- Do you **Beseech?** "Inspire others to join you to do mighty things."

Which leadership/management orientation style do you respond to best?

'RACING THE MORETON WAY'

Each of these different communication 'Orientation Styles were on display in my recent adventure to the breathtaking 'Land Down Under' as a member of a crew in a major 'Americas Cup Class' sailboat race in Australia. Only ten days together, eighteen people, racing a high performance 60 foot Volvo sail boat, competing in the Hamilton Island Regatta - the most prestigious race in Australia.

Only five of us had ever sailed before. Only three of us had ever raced before. Only thirteen of the eighteen people knew one another before agreeing to the trip. Yet it went so smoothly that in the six-day race we won on two of the days - taking 1st place against the 16 boats in our class. We finished second on one day; and took third on two of the other days - racing against faster, bigger, more elaborate, multi-million dollar yachts with professional crews. How did we do it? Four things were apparent:

First: Our sponsor, 'The Moreton Group,' which is the premier Financial Advisors Company in all of Australia, paid for the entire event, assembled our team, and sparred no expense in making us a first class entry. Not only did our incredible hosts Cameron and Jacqueline Dickson buy a new and beautifully 'branded' main sail and graphically designed logo signage to customize our yacht, but they outfitted each of us in matching uniforms, which included special gloves, hats, expensive brand name shoes, shorts, and customized shirts, jackets, and travel bags. Consequently, we looked like champions, which translated into us feeling like champions, which inspired us to compete like champions.

Even the crews of the famous 'Wild Oats' and 'Black Jack' and 'Charlotte' yachts were congratulating us on our world class commitment to excellence, cordial and professional interaction with each of them, and for being the 'tidiest' boat in the inspection. To no one's surprise, at the conclusion of Race Week, our team was honored at the elegant Gala with the prestigious 'Prix d' Elegance' award for 'Best Presented Crew and Yacht' for the entire 233 boat Regatta!

The beautiful silver plate is now proudly displayed in the Moreton office in Brisbane. Yes, we must be the same on task as we are off task – the same at work as we are at home, at school, at play – the same on the water racing as we are off the water socializing - exemplifying the same high moral and ethical character when people are not watching as we do when they are!

Second: When we first climbed aboard the Volvo 60 racing yacht, we were greeted by the amazing Jo who introduced us to her extraordinary partner Mr. Michael Schwarzel of Grand Prix Yachting - the hired, experienced and respected professional sailor whom we now would call 'Skipper.' As a no-nonsense leader Michael immediately began our orientation by explaining each of the job titles and accompanying responsibilities required to sail and race the boat. He then asked each of us to choose what we thought we were best suited for that would help everybody else do their chosen job to the very best of our abilities. In this way we would enthusiastically embrace our strengths, which creates a culture of confidence and supportive synergy, instead of negatively fighting against our weaknesses, which drains our positive energy drip dry!

Third: The Skipper then turned each of us into equal partners with the same expectations by getting every one of us to agree to expect breakdowns. We agreed to expect things to go wrong. Thirteen first-time novice sailors taking a stab at the seas for the sake of adventure meant that we would experience some setbacks - but what made those setbacks bearable, even laughable, was that we communicated about them first.

Saying "we are going to mess up. Can we all agree to accepting this?" with a smile on your face makes the world of a difference. When you acknowledge the possibility of failing and decide that you never really fail or lose if you always learn - it brings play to problems. And don't all of our problems need a little more play, a little more levity, a change in our perception of having a problem (that sounds insurmountable) to accepting a challenge that will bring personal growth?

Fourth: The Skipper conducted an attitude assessment – giving us the proverbial Zig Ziglar 'check up from the neck up to avoid hardening of the attitudes,' reminding us every day that we only had six race days – one at a time - to accomplish our goal of putting in a respectable competitive performance.

The Skipper gave us a weather report at the beginning of each day, acknowledging that on two of the six race days we would be facing 25 to 30 knot winds and huge waves, but not to worry because our Volvo yacht was specifically built for these extreme conditions and all we had to do was do our individual jobs and all would be well. No pressure because we had been trained to do what was necessary. Every new day was a new and fresh chance to prove that our physical strength, mental toughness, spiritual understanding and emotional energy were 'refillable!'

The Skipper was a master at 'transferring trust' through his knowledge and experience to the point we had total confidence in his individual ability and therefore, naturally followed his directions as he communicated in a way where each of us at our different levels of understanding and physical capabilities could understand and respond.

It was obvious that because each of us had an equal part in creating this adventure, we equally supported one another in our attempt to accomplish our collective goals. Which in turn created a deeper connection between us both on and off the boat based on a genuine love and respect for one another as a group of team members who felt valued and appreciated.

And so, the adventure was amazing - not just because the people were amazing, fun loving, positive human brings, but because we also agreed to be a focused, unselfish, respectful, one heart/one mind/single purpose team no matter what - before any negative thing occurred.

EXPECTATIONS

Expectations are first set by everybody in the organization as individual goals to achieve personal excellence. Then, in a collaborative environment of trust, mutual respect and support, each team member shares his/her personal expectations until everybody comes to a consensus on which expectations they will all agree on as the achievement requirements to be part of the team. The agreement is always predicated on the fact they must be 'realistic' based on the current talent and skills level of each individual in the group.

Most important to this process of establishing 'realistic' expectations is the agreement there will be failures and less-than-perfect performances by everyone at some time, so learn from the mistakes and get over it! From a sports perspective, the much quoted confession by basketball super star Michael Jordan is legendary: "I've missed more than 9000 shots in my career. I've lost almost 300 games. 26 times, I've been trusted to take the game winning shot and missed. I've failed over and over and over again in my life. And that is why I succeed." In football, not every play is designed to score a touchdown. In baseball, you can have a .300 batting average, which means you fail or strike out seven out of ten times up to bat, and yet you still make maximum salary as a super star!

CHAPTER TWENTY-ONE

LEADING FROM THE INSIDE OUT

In the following chart of stereotypical differences, which qualities most accurately describe you, and which ones do you need to work on in order to be both a successful manager and a Significant Partner Leader:

- Manager's title is appointed and bestowed / A Leader's title is earned
- Managers are copies / Leaders are original
- Managers administer / Leaders innovate
- Managers maintain / Leaders develop
- Managers accept the status quo / Leaders challenge it.
- Successful managers are Transactional / Successful leaders are Inspirational

SIGNIFICANT PARTNER LEADERS ARE TRANSFORMATIONAL

- Transactional leaders find themselves and create followers.
- **Transformational Partner Leaders** create themselves and produce leaders.
- Transactional leaders are obsessed with position, power, politics and perks.
- **Transformational Partner Leaders** are motivated by purposes, values, morals and ethics.

- Transactional leaders focus on short-term profits, fulfill current job descriptions, supported by existing systems and "human doings" to maximize efficiencies and do things right.
- **Transformational Partner Leaders** focus on long-term objectives, design and re-design roles that are relevant and meaningful, supported by overarching values and "human beings" to maximize effectiveness and do the right things.
- Transactional leaders take credit when the team succeeds and give blame when it fails.
- **Transformational Partner Leaders** give credit to the team when they win and take blame when they lose.
- Transactional leaders create & maintain a small, exclusive "inner circle of safety," where they willingly sacrifice others for the benefit of themselves.
- **Transformational Partner Leaders** create and maintain a large, all-inclusive "circle of safety," where they willingly sacrifice themselves for the benefit of others.

CHAPTER TWENTY-TWO

LEADING THROUGH PERSUASION

MOVING NEEDS TO WANTS AND WHY TO HOW

For decades, the most popular old school sales program was called Needs Satisfaction Selling, which proclaimed: "the customer is king and always right." When we identify his/her Needs we can accommodate them with our product and service.

We now know this is obsolete. For example, if you live in a snow belt and Need a vacation to get out of the cold, any tropical destination can satisfy your Need. This is good for you, the customer, because competition among hot beach locations drives the cost down. However, low prices and a consumer's Need to get more for less is bad for travel destinations, adventure tours and hotels that service them.

If you are taking your wife to a black tie gala and she Needs a new pair of black stilettos to match her gown, any brand of formal shoes can solve her dilemma.

However, if you WANT to treat your family to a two-week, $25,000 vacation in Jaco, Costa Rica, or for your 25th wedding anniversary, take your sweetheart on a 30-day $ 30,000 exotic cruise from Fort Lauderdale, Florida to Buenos Aires, Argentina and onto Antarctica aboard a magnificent Seabourn Luxury Liner, then you'll pay these outrageous prices because the alternatives simply don't meet your expectations, nor do they achieve your desired results.

And if your wife WANTS a pair of $2,445 Christian Louboutin Maralena Heels, with the French designer's signature trademarked red-lacquered sole that can be seen from far away, that hordes of Hollywood starlets have been seen sporting at award shows, premieres and red carpet events, then the crazy and unconscionable high price is suddenly acceptable and reasonable. If she Wants those shoes, she won't be satisfied with any substitution. In fact, the high prices actually fuel her motivation to buy them, because everybody knows how much they cost and WANT them too!

These high-priced examples are purposefully chosen to compare and contrast the mindset of one of the wealthiest people in the world, Warren Buffett. At a net worth of $65.2 billion, he doesn't Need to impress anybody. He simply Wants to live in a small home in a modest neighborhood in Omaha, Nebraska because of the quality of life he Wants to live! Ironically, this also illustrates that when it comes to Need and Want, money is seldom a factor, regardless of our net worth. Even when Mr. Buffett stays at The Four Seasons in New York City, he still Wants his favorite foods: a 6-dollar combo Cherry Coke, Dairy Queen Burger, and Blizzard dessert! Ironically, this also illustrates that when it comes to Needs and Wants, money is seldom a factor.

What causes this? Brand Value. Value is always determined by what we are willing to give up in order to get it. This means the amount of money is irrelevant if the perceived value of creating a specific memory with your family outweighs the cost. Or the perceived value of purchasing a specific pair of shoes gives your wife a sense of sophisticated elegance as part of the glamorous Hollywood jet set. Or the perceived taste of a specific food satisfies your craving. The desire for the brand - the Want - is what makes the memory, product, service, and food most valuable.

This means that instead of spending your time and hard-earned resources on convincing your associates and/or potential customers WHY they should follow your advice and/or buy your product and service, you can use your time and energy showing them how they can stay fully engaged with you and your business.

When you get people to choose YOU, not just someone who does what you do, you will find that the entire process of influence and/or sales cycle quickens and strengthens, while the How-To becomes the obvious urgent series of next steps to reaching the mutually agreed upon desired outcome results.

CHAPTER TWENTY-THREE

LEADING WITH STYLE AND EXPECTATIONS

"SITUATIONAL LEADERSHIP"

- **DIRECTING** – telling; giving instructions to be followed here and now.
- **COACHING** – demonstrating; allowing learning by doing.
- **SUPPORTING** – sharing; referring to resources; giving positive reinforcement.
- **DELEGATING** – watching; letting others do it with minimal supervision.

Which is your dominant style? Which (if any) of the other three styles do you subscribe to?

Your answer becomes your foundation for developing and becoming proficient in the other three leadership styles. Because of our diverse work force, gender differences, varying individual learning styles, and thick or thin-skinned personalities, when the circumstance and the individuals with whom we are working change, our leadership style must change to meet the needs of the moment. On September 10, 2001, New York City Mayor Rudy Giuliani was most likely using his dominant communication style to take care of business that day. However, when the terrorist planes hit the World Trade Center the following morning, he was suddenly required to use all four styles, sometimes changing in an instant.

Significant Partner Leadership is not a step-by-step program list of things to do, but rather a condition of the heart based on

Predictable Trust. Leaders don't seek to control, they liberate. The fruits of an exceptional leader appear predominantly among the followers. Are the subordinates reaching their full potential? Are they learning and serving? Do the followers understand and accept diversity? Can they manage conflict? When they trust you to teach/show them, they can and will rise to the occasion as they have seen you do.

Which style do you respond to best? Why? Regardless of your current 'Orientation' and natural 'Leadership Style' the one communication technique and tool we all must perfect is the art of individually connecting through Expectations.

'FAIR' IS NOT ALWAYS 'EQUAL'

As a diehard fan of the Utah Jazz – my professional hometown team in National Basketball Association, I attended the majority of the games back in the hay-day seasons watching Hall of Fame super star players John Stockton and Karl Malone. I even traveled back and forth to Chicago to watch both the 1997 and the 1998 NBA Finals games to cheer on my Jazz against Michael Jordan and his Chicago Bulls. Living in the same neighborhood with Karl Malone and his amazing wife Kay, I had become friends with several of the Jazz players and with legendary Head Coach Frank Layden.

Having several chances to watch practice, I had the opportunity to witness the work ethic of every player on the Jazz and watch and listen to how the coaches interacted with them. What always fascinated me was how differently they communicated with each player – especially the super stars Stockton and Malone.

These experiences would turn out to be the perfect point of reference in a future four-hour interview I had with Coach Layden. The opportunity to pick his brain was life changing for me because he is one of the only coaches in history who not only coached a professional team to win several Conference Championships, but he has won championships coaching at the high school level and at the college/university level. For this reason, he was uniquely qualified to ask if there was one common denominator that made him extraordinarily successful, regardless of the age of the players and the sophistication of the program.

Coach Layden's answer was a profound lesson in leadership that taught me three major truths. He said, "Fair is not necessarily equal. Every player on the team has different needs at different times for different reasons. Sometimes this player needs more attention than that player and requires that I focus more of my time and energy on him right now than the other players."

Coach Layden then taught me the second truth using the two different personalities of Stockton and Malone as the perfect example. He said if he yelled at Malone in an attempt to motivate him and increase his work ethic and productivity, and told Karl he was 'loafing' and lazy and not worth the money he was being paid, Karl would have put his head down, considered quitting, felt humiliated, walked out of practice angry at the coach, and would have given less effort in their next practice and game. Yelling at Karl and getting in his face would have a reverse effect on his productivity and actually backfire as a motivator.

Coach Layden continued, "To inspire and motivate Karl Malone to increase his performance, I had to put my arm around him and compliment him for his talent and hard work, and then suggest that he could actually go down in the history books as the greatest 'Power Forward" ever to play professional basketball if he will just think this way, do this thing, and put in this much extra time."

Coach continued, "On the other hand, if I yelled at John Stockton for 'loafing' and got in his face, threatening to sit him on the bench if he didn't work harder, Stockton would have gotten angry at himself, with an intense rebuttal, "Are you serious? How dare you accuse me of not giving it my all! I work harder than anyone on the team, and if you don't think so, watch what I do today!"

Coach Layden told me that Malone only responds to compliments and encouragement and kindness and positive reinforcement, followed by suggestions on how to improve, knowing he is loved and wanted and appreciated and needed. However, if you try to put your arm around Stockton and try to love him into increasing his performance, he becomes suspicious and blows you off without taking you seriously.

Notice that Stockton and Malone have the exact same emotional needs and share the exact same desired end result and team goal of winning the championship. And, the depth level of trust in both of their relationships with Coach Layden was the same. Yet the way Coach Layden went about inspiring them to motivate themselves to do whatever it takes to win was totally different – all based on personality. He definitely treated them both equally fair, but different.

'EQUAL EXPECTATIONS' ALWAYS MAKE IT 'FAIR'

Coach then taught me the third leadership truth referring to the "Rock Foundational Beliefs," positive mental attitude, and desired behaviors that never change – that are at the heart and soul of creating the desired 'Partner Leadership Culture.' Regardless if the team member is the highest paid, multi-year contracted, 'franchise player' on the roster or the lowest paid 'journeyman' with a one-year minimum salary deal, every player and person in the organization is held to the same standards as everybody else. These agreed upon performance standards are obviously only the 'minimum requirement' starting points that we refer to as 'Expectations.'

CHAPTER TWENTY-FOUR

LEADING THROUGH COVENANT SERVICE

COMMITMENTS AND COVENANTS

A commitment is a two-way contract born out of suspicion. I will make a list of my responsibilities and you will make a list of your responsibilities. I will hold you accountable for your list and you will hold me accountable for my list. If either one of us violate any part of the commitment agreement and fall short of our expected performance on any one of the line items on the lists, the contract is broken and void.

In contrast, a covenant is a one-way promise born out of trust to engage in or refrain from a specified action. In other words, what you think, say, or do does not change the principles and core values by which I govern my life, nor does it change the way I treat you ethically and morally. I don't love and respect you as a human being because of what you have done or who you are. I love and respect you because of who I am; and who I am knows those wrapped up in them selves make a small package.

The best illustration of this came from my friend 'DDP' Diamond Dallas Page, the former three-time WWE World Wrestling Champion. He grew up in New Jersey and has huge celebrity connections. One day I was riding in the back seat of his SUV when his phone rang. I wasn't ease dropping but apparently someone he knew wanted Dallas to get him some great tickets to Bruce Springsteen's concert and backstage passes. Dallas said, 'Call this guy, go hear, tell him I'll cover for you, and then go there and everything will be perfect.'

When Dallas hung up from the call his wife Kimberly blurted, 'I can't believe he just called you. Why are you always so nice to him? All he ever does is use you!' To which Dallas replied, 'Why should I let what someone says or how they treat me change who I am as a man, or lower the high standards of class and service before self that I've established for myself?'

Bam! Oh how I love and admire Dallas Page! As is the case in everything in life, before we can expect someone else to do something we must first embrace it and fully engage in doing it ourselves – especially when it comes to making a covenant to service before self often referred to as 'servant leadership.' There are four categorical ways in which we can and should personally covenant to serve:

- Serve just to serve, when and where others won't.
- Serve out of duty, honor, and gratitude.
- Serve your organization in a way that allows your teammates to accomplish more with you than without you.
- Serve a cause larger than yourself.

PERSONAL COVENANT

A prominent local businessman frequently brought his clients to a posh hotel to hold lunch meetings in the lobby restaurant. One day he showed up with his young son. When the boy excused himself to go to the washroom the General Manager asked the father what the special occasion was. The father sadly reported that his son had been diagnosed with cancer and that the next morning he would start his brutal chemotherapy treatment.

Father and son were spending the night and after their dinner, a dip in the pool, and a movie, his son was going to shave his head to prepare for the morning ordeal. Dad said his son knew he was going to lose his hair anyway and thought that by shaving it, he would be taking a more positive, proactive approach to fighting his cancer and controlling it instead of letting it control him. Dad explained that he too, was going to shave his head in a sign of unconditional loving solidarity.

The father then asked the Manager for a special favor, requesting that when they appeared the following morning for breakfast, that the wait staff did not react openly to their shaved heads or inquire about the reason they were both bald, for fear of embarrassing his son at what was to be the start of the most challenging period of his life. When they arrived for breakfast, nobody in the room batted an eyelid nor said a word. Four of the waiters, however, had also shaved their heads that night too.

PROFESSIONAL COVENANT

When you are starting and building any kind of business, especially an extraordinary career as a Significant Sales Professional, establishing a culture of covenant service is critical to attracting the right coworkers, support staff and customers, who together believe what you believe.

Remember, significant organizations and significant individuals are measured exclusively by what their larger purpose is – why they exist? In the world of sales and maintaining loyal venders, suppliers and customers, "Cause Marketing" is the proven formula to deepen relationships at every level.

Cone/Roper released a five-year study that reveals the highlights and power of 'cause marketing':

- Overall, corporate responsibility and citizenship remain highly valued by Americans. Incorporating a number of business practices in support of a cause helps demonstrate a company's commitment and enhances its credibility.

- Eight in ten Americans have a more positive image of companies that support a cause they care about.

- Nearly two-thirds of Americans agree that cause programs should be a standard business practice.

- More than 60 percent of consumers will switch retailers if they support the same cause the consumer supports.

- Nine in ten workers feel a greater sense of pride and a stronger sense of loyalty to their companies with cause programs, which translates into enhanced customer service and positive word of mouth.

- More than half of all employees wish their employers would do more to support a social cause.

- Eighty-seven percent of employees of companies with cause programs wish their companies would measure success in social as well as financial terms.

CHAPTER TWENTY-FIVE

LEADING WITH A MILITARY MINDSET

An MBA gives you tools and familiarity, but it doesn't put you in a real-world situation. An MBA teaches the analytical side, military teaches the people management - expectation - execution side. Military Officers/NCOs have been schooled, tutored, and tested in Twelve Principles of Leadership:

- Know yourself and seek continuous self-improvement
- Be technically and tactically proficient
- Seek responsibility and take responsibility for your actions
- Make sound and timely decisions
- Set the example
- Know your troops by name and look out for their wellbeing
- Keep your subordinates informed
- Develop a sense of responsibility in your subordinates
- Ensure that each assigned task is understood, supervised and accomplished
- Employ your unit only in accordance with its training and capabilities
- Know your enemy
- Never demand and order 'go' - always command and encourage 'follow me'

Young Officers and Senior NCOs manage large teams and multi-million dollar budgets at an age when the majority of their peers are taking the first steps on their career paths. And let us not forget that the hardest thing to teach up and coming managers is the value of developing and training strong subordinate leaders, which is simply part of everyday military culture.

All in all, it is obvious that "book smart" doesn't hold a candle to "street smart" experience. The essence of being a military leader is to figure out how to deploy forces and resources to get something done, based on a sense of mission, clearly focused objectives, and knowing what constitutes success and failure.

CHAPTER TWENTY-SIX

LEADING WITH A 'CREED'

The elite few known as the Army Rangers, who along with the Navy SEALS (as in Marcus Luttrell, whose story is told in the movie Lone Survivor, and Team 6, who killed Osama bin Laden), Delta Force, and the Special Forces Green Berets constitute the world's most highly trained and feared warriors.

The Ranger Creed illustrates what all these special men have in common: a nearly incomprehensible obedience and an unselfish commitment to loyalty, duty, respect, service before self, honor, country, integrity and personal courage.

As you read the Creed, ask yourself if you are man or woman enough to hold yourself to this same high standard of ethical excellence in all you do, and if that level of ethical excellence exists within your organization.

My young neighbor, U.S. Army Lt. Ben Westman (whom I coached in football for six years), graduated from the U.S. Military Academy at West Point. During his senior year Ben served as one of only thirty-two Company Commanders. After graduation, Ben headed for an intensely grueling two months of Ranger School, affectionately called "No Excuses Leadership Training."

Each day candidates spend long hours hiking, running, and swimming in full combat gear. They sleep in the field and eat two fewer meals a day than normal, losing twenty to thirty pounds by the time the training concludes. Although most candidates don't make it through this school on their first attempt, Ben passed with flying colors and upon graduation proudly committed to obey the Ranger Creed:

THE UNITED STATES ARMY RANGER CREED

"**R**ecognizing that I volunteered as a Ranger, fully knowing the hazards of my chosen profession, I will always endeavor to uphold the prestige, honor, and high esprit de corps of my Rangers Regiment.

"**A**cknowledging the fact that a Ranger is a more elite Soldier who arrives at the cutting edge of battle by land, sea, or air, I accept the fact that as a Ranger, my country expects me to move further, faster and fight harder than any other Soldier.

"**N**ever shall I fail my comrades. I will always keep myself mentally alert, physically strong and morally straight, and I will shoulder more than my share of the task, whatever it may be, 100 hundred percent and then some.

"**G**allantly will I show the world that I am a specially selected and well-trained Soldier? My courtesy to superior officers, neatness of dress and care of equipment shall set the example for others to follow.

“**E**nergetically will I meet the enemies of my country. I shall defeat them on the field of battle, for I am better trained and will fight with all my might. Surrender is not a Ranger word. I will never leave a fallen comrade to fall into the hands of the enemy, and under no circumstances will I ever embarrass my country.

“**R**eadily will I display the intestinal fortitude required to fight on to the Ranger objective and complete the mission, though I be the lone survivor.”

These are not mere words. Just before Ben left for his 12 month deployment, leading and fighting side by side with his men in the mountains of Afghanistan, he left me with his proud and intense war call, “Rangers lead the way,” and a quote by Steven Press field that gave me a greater sense of how Rangers think, feel, prepare, and thrive in their high-performance world:

> *“When a warrior fights not for himself, but for his brothers; when his most passionately sought goal is neither glory nor his own life’s preservation, but to spend his substance for them, his comrades; not to abandon them, not to prove unworthy of them; then his heart has truly achieved contempt for death; and with that he transcends himself, and his actions touch the sublime.”*

All specialized weapons, survival, and combat readiness programs re-quire and instill extreme fitness, yet these elite fighting men realize a greater purpose and a more comprehensive residual benefit while pushing themselves to their ultimate capacity and potential.

Consequently, it is no surprise that my young friend, Army Ranger Ben Westman, continues to push himself to his limits as he has now been promoted to captain and completed the eighteen-month, invitation only, Special Forces Training at Ft. Bragg, North Carolina.

What personal creed do you live by, and what credos do you have in your organization to inspire this level of sacrifice, unity, hard work, and love?

Every corporation and organization should be so lucky as to have a former military officer/SNCO as the CEO or COO to lead them! So if you are not, what will you do to become one in your current job description and industry? Remember, you can lead without a title.

Because we become the average of the five people we associate with the most, I challenge you to become the civilian equivalent to an Army Ranger, Navy Seal, Delta Force, and Special Forces Green Be-ret – who will inspire others to become more of who they already are by subscribing to a higher expectation and personal covenant/creed?

A MILITARY BAND OF BROTHERS

"We few, we happy few, we band of brothers. For he today that sheds his blood with me shall be my brother; be never so vile. This day shall gentle his condition. And gentlemen in England now abed shall think themselves accursed they were not here, and hold their man hoods cheap whiles any speaks that fought with us upon Saint Crispin's day."— Shakespeare

On the cold morning of April 6, 2008, Captain Kyle Walton was tasked with the dangerous mission of taking his elite team of warriors into the remote Afghan terrorist stronghold of the notorious HIG militant group. At the crack of dawn, this 12-man U.S. Special Forces team (sometimes called the Green Berets), and 20 U.S. trained Afghan commandos, each carrying 60 to 80 pounds of gear, were lowered out of helicopters onto sharp, ice-covered rocks and into freezing water at an altitude of 10,000 feet.

As they made their way up the steep mountain terrain toward a cluster of thick-walled mud buildings, the insurgents scrambled to their fighting positions and for the next seven hours, unloaded a barrage of machine gun fire, relentless sniper fire and countless rocket-propelled grenades onto the exposed soldiers - shooting at each of the U.S. positions from virtually all sides. As hundreds of bullets ricocheted off the rocks, two rounds slammed into Walton's helmet, smashing his head into the ground.

Immediately an Afghan interpreter was killed. Staff Sergeant Luis Morales was shot in the right thigh and Staff Sergeant Dillon Behr was hit in the hip. Morales and Walton pulled Behr back to their position where Morales cut open Behr's pants and applied pressure to his bleeding wound. Moments later, Morales was hit again, in the ankle, leaving him struggling to treat himself and his comrade.

Suddenly Staff Sergeant John Wayne Walding was hit below his right knee, and saw that the bullet amputated his right leg. What would you have done? Walding grabbed his boot and put it in his crotch, then grabbed the boot laces and tied it to his thigh, so it would not flop around while he continued to shoot at the bad guys and help his brothers win the fight. There was about two inches of meat holding his leg on, so he put on a tourniquet and watched the blood flow out the stump to see when it was tight enough.

When asked why and how he was able to persevere, he smiled and proudly replied, "My name is John Wayne, so I had to stay engaged in the fight!"

A round suddenly hit Staff Sgt. Ford in the chest, knocking him back but not penetrating his body armor. A minute later, another bullet went through his left arm and shoulder, hitting the helmet of the medic, Staff Sgt. Ronald J. Shurer, who was behind him treating Behr. An insurgent sniper was zeroing in on them and they had to make a serious move or clearly they would die.

Bleeding heavily from the arm, Staff Stg. Ford put together a plan to begin removing the wounded and radioed in for Air Force jets to begin dropping bombs on enemy positions. The evacuation plan was that every time they dropped a bomb, they would move down the steep cliffs until they made their way to the streambed, with those who could still walk carrying the wounded.

A Medevac helicopter flew in, but because of the relentless barrage of bullets coming from the enemy, the pilot hovered just long enough for the medic to jump off, and then flew away. Another helicopter came in, but was forced down in the middle of the fast-moving river, where it took two or three men to carry each of the wounded to safety. As they took off under heavy fire, a bullet grazed the pilot's head. At battle's end, two Afghan Commandos were killed, and the Green Berets had suffered fifteen wounded, while an estimated two hundred insurgents were dead.

TEN SILVER STARS / ONE AIR FORCE CROSS

For their bravery under fire, Walton and his nine soldiers received the Silver Star Medal—the third highest military decoration awarded for valor and gallantry in action against an enemy of the United States.

In addition to the Army soldiers being decorated for their bravery, Senior Airman Zachary Rhyner, ODA 3336's Air Force Combat Controller, was awarded the Air Force Cross, the second-highest military award that can be given to a member of the United States Air Force, recognizing extraordinary heroism shown in combat.

During the battle Rhyner was shot twice in the chest and once in the leg, although his protective vest stopped the two bullets to his chest from causing a mortal injury. Despite being wounded within the first fifteen minutes of the battle, Rhyner continued to direct close air support and airstrikes until the assault force was evacuated seven hours later.

Fifty of the airstrikes he called in were within 200 meters of friendly positions (the term "danger close" is applied when referring to airstrikes within 600 meters). Rhyner was credited with saving the entire 100-man team from being overrun twice.

When asked in an interview why and how they were able to overcome the massive odds and live to fight another day, Walding said it best, "We intensified our 'Situational Awareness,' obeyed our instincts and lived our Special Forces Creed, which allowed us to trust our training and fight for each other as a true band of brothers!"

This heroic experience reminds us of General Douglass MacArthur's words, "If we sweat more in peace we will bleed less in war. On the fields of friendly strife are sown the seeds that on other days and other fields will bear the fruits of victory."

Life lessons learned? When we are prepared we shall not fear. When we learn and practice the Partner Leadership character traits of humility, self-discipline, sacrifice and service before self in a non-emotional environment, we prepare ourselves and guarantee that we will display extraordinary leadership and courage when thrown into an extremely emotional environment. Why? How? Partner Leaders believe, exemplify and inspire others to live by the words of Actor John Wayne: "Courage is when you are scared to death and you saddle up anyway!"

The thing that saved these brave and courageous soldiers and Airman Rhyner was their 'Covenant Conviction' to their 'Creeds.' It didn't matter what was happening to who. As partners each of them needed to rise to the occasion, step up to the task at hand, lead without a title or special Army rank, and serve and fight to live. In this mindset a Partner Leader is a leader who knows that you don't judge a man when he is up – you judge him when he is down, because you will never meet a strong man or woman with a weak past. Partner Leaders know it's not what happens to you that defines who you are. It's what you do with what happens to you that defines who you are – especially when you are doing it for someone else.

CHAPTER TWENTY-SEVEN

LEADING WITH SIGNIFICANT CONNECTIONS

THE 'SOFT POWER' OF THE UNITED STATES AIR FORCE

I proudly serve as a member of the International Board of Governors of Operation Smile, a humanitarian organization whose plastic surgeons and critical care pediatric nurses volunteer their time to perform cleft lip and palate surgeries on underprivileged, needy children throughout the world.

My favorite Operation Smile experience happened in Iraq, where our team planned to operate on 110 Iraqi children who had severe facial deformities, including twenty-nine under the age of two. A mission was organized to transport the children with their parents, medical volunteers, and nine Iraqi doctors (210 people total) across the desert in several buses on a twenty-four-hour ride to Amman, Jordan.

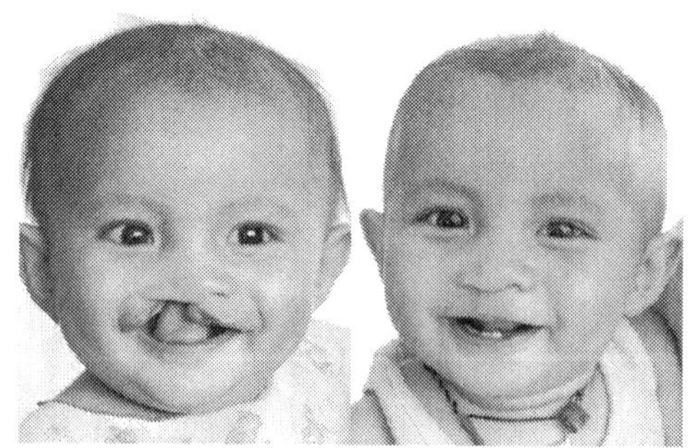

Halfway there, terrorist insurgents boarded the buses, screaming, pointing guns and knives, and demanding that any of the rival religious faction be identified and dragged off the buses to be executed. No one responded. Miraculously, thirty minutes later, the terrorists got off the buses without hurting anyone and disappeared into the night. The frightened Iraqi families and medical volunteers continued to Amman, and within days, the 110 surgeries had been successfully completed.

All 210 people on this mission were terrified at the idea of making the long bus ride home. Even the bus drivers refused to go. I received a phone call from my dear friend Michael Nebeker, whose sister Susan was on this mission and had reported the details to him over the phone. Then the co-founders of Operation Smile, Dr. Bill Magee and his wife Kathy, called to see if I could use my relationship with the US Air Force to help.

I had just spoken at the World Command Chiefs Conference for my friend and hero Gerald Murray, Command Chief Master Sergeant of the Air Force, so I phoned him right after hanging up with Dr. Magee. Knowing how important it is for the United States to win hearts and minds with "soft power," Murray said he could get this thing done if we generated a "sponsor letter" from a senator or congressman. Senator John Warner (R-Virginia) and Congressman Trent Franks (D-Arizona), with the incredible support from my dear friend Senator Orrin Hatch (R-Utah), composed the letter and then hand-delivered it to Defense Secretary Rumsfeld.

Chief Murray then counseled with Air Force chief of staff General T. Michael Moseley, and within twenty-four hours, two C-17 transport jets were sent from Baghdad to Amman to rescue these 210 people. When they landed safely at the Baghdad International Airport, the families and medical volunteers walked down the stairs with their now beautiful babies and brand-new smiles.

They knelt down in thanksgiving to kiss the ground of their homeland, and then stood to cheer and thank the military men and women who had loved them and unselfishly served them that day.

Clearly, Dr. Bill and Kathy Magee are international angels of love, hope, mercy, and medical miracles. Operation Smile creates medical diplomacy everywhere it goes and epitomizes what it means to be an international citizen of the world. Learn how to get involved at www.operationsmile.org, and discover how both the giver and the receiver of covenant service are transformed from successful to significant.

CHAPTER TWENTY-EIGHT

LEADING THROUGH THE WILDERNESS

YOU DON'T GO INTO THE WILDERNESS - YOU GO THROUGH THE WILDERNESS

Throughout history, it seems that all great leaders have had a wilderness experience—a significant emotional event away from life as they know it, where they have to ask tough questions and discover who they are, why they are, and what matters most to them during a time of self-actualization when they focus and finely tune their thoughts and cleanse their souls.

Going into our wilderness is not an experience of failure but rather a moment of truth, a wake-up call, a do-or-die experience of refinement that takes us to a place we cannot take ourselves—a place not occupied by what happens to us but by the lessons we are learning and by what we are doing with what happens to us.

Such experiences are always therapeutic and life affirming, and they remind us of Native American wisdom: "All answers are in the forest" or, as I put it, "The answers are in the box - everything that is required to take ourselves to the next level is already inside us."

The wilderness is an intense inside-out, internal excavating, self-audit experience that teaches us that in life there are no mistakes, only lessons—lessons taught not by how we react but by how we respond. Reaction is negative, like an adverse reaction to medication. Responding is positive, such as when your body responds to the medication and you get well.

Robert Frost explained it best when he said, "The best way out is through." For example, every day in Calcutta, India, a once-poor, homeless, and starving woman takes manure, molds it into small patties, and sells them or trades them for food and other necessities of life. Her customers burn the patties for heat and cooking, and she has shelter and a better life. We too can do as the peasant woman does and use the pain in our lives to rise above our social and financial predicaments and make our dreams come true.

We too can decide there is never a good time to quit. Failing our way to success is requisite to becoming significant. We all need a setback before we can have a comeback. Only those who fail, fall, sacrifice, and go without are humble and contrite enough to learn the deepest, most meaningful lessons: that when we hit a wall or make a mistake, we always look at it as a wilderness experience—not as an end but as a new beginning; not as a closed door but as an open door.

Bottom line. The greatest leaders in history all share the common leadership thread of 'Resiliency.' U.S. President Teddy Roosevelt lost his wife and his mother on the same day. Franklin D. Roosevelt flunked out of Columbia Law School because he wasn't smart enough and later had to battle and deal with his polio. Basketball superstar Michael Jordan was cut from his high school basketball team as a fifteen-year-old kid because he wasn't good enough.

How did they respond? As we share three powerful examples, notice how the individuals go through the wilderness, not into it. The wilderness refines us.

MAHATMA

Mahatma Gandhi came from a wealthy family and was the pride of his parents. He had every advantage—the best schools, a law degree, and an introduction to important people. But he had to prove himself a capable lawyer without the help and influence of his family's social standing. In the courtroom in India, Gandhi presented a terrible image of himself. He was too frightened to stand up to his opposition and was easily overwhelmed.

As he reached his lowest, most wretched level of suffering and realized that he would never become a prominent attorney, he took his outward challenges and turned them into an inward wilderness experience that took him from India to South Africa, where he spent twenty years as an expatriate in nonviolent resistance to England. There, Gandhi was with people who were worse off than he was, and he realized that his homeland could also use some help.

In the moments of suffering during his worst failures, Gandhi looked at himself, didn't like what he saw, saw others more down and out than he, and developed his own passive nonresistance philosophy that led him back to his native India to lead his people to independence from British rule.

MICKEY?

Inside a cold, damp garage in the Midwest sat a struggling, half-starved illustrator trying to make a living with his pictures. As he sat there in his wilderness, exerting his brain for inspiration, a mouse ran across his foot. Generally speaking, mice smell up the place, are not welcome, make a nuisance of them selves, and are afraid of humans.

The young illustrator watched the mouse boldly walk, almost strut, into the hole in the wall as he thought about how hungry and lonely he was and how miserable his chances were of succeeding as an artist. "The mouse doesn't even respect me," he thought. "Why should I respect myself?"

At his lowest, most humble point, he began to imagine what that confident, pesky, perky mouse was like, and he began to draw and develop its personality. America and the world have never been the same since that unknown mouse, who was quickly named Mickey, ran across the foot of that discouraged, unknown illustrator named Walt Disney.

ABE

U.S. President Abraham Lincoln's string of failures is documented and much talked about, validating that failure is usually the first step toward success—if we are not failing a few times, we are not pushing ourselves hard enough. What made Lincoln significant was his ability to read himself, which enabled him to read others. His greatest quality and character trait was his remarkable power of self-reflection. Self-reflection can only be learned and perfected in the wilderness.

Unlike the examples of Gandhi and Disney, Lincoln's wilderness experience was not chosen or thrust upon him in adulthood. When Lincoln was just three years old, his newborn younger brother died.

When he was nine, Abe's mother, aunt, and uncle died. His sister died in childbirth when he was eighteen. Lincoln battled anxiety and depression his entire life, leading to his tendency to melancholy.

In his twenties, Abe struggled with identity issues. He had no real formal education, but by studying grammar and reading the daily newspapers while working as postmaster in his township, he acquired knowledge and political conviction, and he learned the rhythms of language. In speeches before the New Salem debate club, he honed his orator's voice.

But against this backdrop of self-discovery came discouragement and failure that would have destroyed most. Lincoln lost his first job at Denton Offutt's store, went bankrupt as partner in the successor store, and was unlucky in love with Ann Rutledge. The middle part of Lincoln's life was spent in Springfield, Illinois, where he became a successful, self-made lawyer, but still he faced identity issues, abruptly breaking off his engagement to Mary Todd.

But again, through self-reflection, Lincoln helped his friend Joshua Speed deal with similar apprehensions about marriage and in the process learned what he needed to be and do to reconnect with Mary a year later. In the last part of Lincoln's life, we know he lost election after election and that even after he became president, no one had a steeper learning curve or brought a slimmer resume.

Lincoln gradually grew into the great man who would save his country. He developed supreme confidence in his faculties. He was ambitious and persistent. Above all, he was a lifelong learner who never stopped asking questions and seeking better answers. From this essential element came his capacity to welcome adversity as a refiner's fire and to continuously persevere, knowing nothing happens 'to' us, everything happens 'for' us, to give us experience for our own good!

PAIN IS A SIGNAL TO GROW, NOT TO SUFFER. ONCE WE LEARN THE LESSON THE PAIN IS TEACHING US, THE PAIN GOES AWAY

Most people go through adverse times, and having the resilience and self-reflection to grow from those tough times is critical. Specific to the Presidents of the United States, when they encountered stress in office, they found effective ways to face it and put it aside.

Abraham Lincoln was able to go to the theater more than 100 times during the Civil War. President Teddy Roosevelt managed to block his calendar to exercise 2 hours every afternoon. President Franklin D. Roosevelt had a cocktail hour every night, where the rule during World War II was you could not talk about the War for those two hours.

These Presidents also had to find ways to control their emotions, which required creative solutions that were unique to them. Lincoln wrote 'hot letters' to people when he was mad at them, and then put the letter aside, hoping he would cool down psychologically and not need to send it. When FDR was angry at a Congressman or Senator, and was required to write his weekly 'Fireside Chats,' he would write terrible things about the person in Draft #1. But by Draft #4 he had calmed down and it was all sweetness and light. He got it out of his system.

Are your 'Rock Foundational Beliefs" strong enough for you to be resilient no matter what? Are you willing to be 'Self-Reflective' long enough to learn the lessons the pain is teaching you so the pain goes away? Do you have coping systems in place to keep things in proper positive perspective? Significant Partner Leaders know you never loose if you always learn!

CHAPTER TWENTY-NINE

LEADING IN THE FAMILY

"No other success can compensate for failure in the home"

Raising significant children is the most important assignment and 'calling' a parent has! Thank heaven it is not complicated, but rather simple. Oftentimes not easy, but always simple because it's only about attitude, quality time, example, opportunity, respect, encouragement, unconditional love and support. For this reason, from the time they were born, every night as I tucked my children in bed, I conditioned their moldable minds with positive thoughts and confidence building affirmations that would illuminate their potential. When they were old enough to have memorized it, I had them repeat it every night before I turned out their lights asking, "Who are you?" Each of them recited back to me what I call the:

CLARK CREDO

I'm smart, talented, and I never say never.
I'm wanted, important, loveable, capable, and I can succeed.
I'm athletic, I love music, and I'll get good grades in school.
If I get knocked down or fall, I just get back up and go again.
If I spill, break something, or make a mistake, I'll learn why, clean it up and say 'no big deal.'
I never say 'I can't. I always say 'I can, I will.'
I love God and He loves me, so I will treat others how I want to be treated,
So when we're apart, we always say, 'I like me best
when I'm with you – I want to see you again.'

Although my children are now adults, to this day they still remember this Clark Credo, can recite it word verbatim, and continue to testify of the positive impact it had on their attitudes and behaviors growing up. The following lyric to a hit song by the same name illustrates a father's responsibility to take parenting to the next level:

SPECIAL MAN

A little boy wants to be like his dad
So he watches us night and day
He mimics our moves and weighs our words
He steps in our steps all the way
He's sculpting a life we're the models for
He'll follow us happy or sad.
And his future depends on example set
Cause the little boy wants to be just like his dad

A special man talks by example
Takes the time to play and hug his lad
A special man walks by example
The very best friend a growing boy ever had
Any male can be a father
But it takes a special man to be a dad

He needs a hero to emulate
He breathes, "I believe in you"
Would we have him see everything we see
And have him do what we do
When we see the reverence that sparkles and shines
In the worshipping eyes of our lad
Will we be at peace if his dreams come true
And he grows up to be just like his dad

A special man talks by example
Takes the time to play and hug his lad
A special man walks by example
The very best friend a growing boy ever had

Any male can be a father
But it takes a special man to be a dad
— Dan Clark copyright 2000

CHAPTER THIRTY

SIGNIFICANT LEADERSHIP AND SIGNIFICANT WEALTH

The success and significance of a team is only a reflection of the people on the team. We have under-performing teams because we have underperforming leaders who have attracted under-performing human beings. Because the mind, body, and spirit constitute the soul of humanity, high-performing leaders create significance by simultaneously and consistently engaging IQ - Intelligence Quotient, EQ - Emotional Quotient, and VQ - Values Quotient.

THE SIGNIFICANT LEADERSHIP MODEL

Of all the requirements facing leaders today, the key question is how do we get people from different philosophies, political views, job descriptions, and levels of authority to follow us and respond to our requests? The answer lies in an understanding of the Significant Leadership Model. Using only common sense and the obvious order of things, may I point out that leadership is a four-pronged proposition that must absolutely extend in all four directions.

We must go inside ourselves to internally excavate who we are and tune up what we believe. That makes leading ourselves and others an automatic subconscious, scientifically proven, proactive way of thinking and living.

IQ (INTELLIGENCE QUOTIENT) has been the traditional and predominant measuring stick of success in school, and a cause for prestigious job placements after graduation. We need to be lifelong learners. Knowledge is power, and being bright is the single most attractive quality in anyone.

EQ (EMOTIONAL QUOTIENT) links strongly to all of the intangible qualities of significance, reassuring us about love, spirituality, service, the capabilities people possess, and the fact that everybody has value. This brings compassion and humanity to work through empathy, vision, and integrity. They say "IQ" gets you the job, but "EQ" is what gets you the promotion, creates job satisfaction, solidifies job security, and makes you stand out in a crowd.

Daniel Goleman popularized this breakthrough in his 1995 book Emotional Intelligence. According to the research, success requires both IQ and the attitudinal, behavioral, and maximizing-potential of EQ, which increases stability, continuity, and harmony in relationships.

For instance, we have all met brilliant people with academic honors who are socially and interpersonally inept as well as unsuccessful in business. They are never looked at as leaders. On the other hand, we also know those who are street savvy and common sense smart, whose only degree is from the school of hard knocks. Yet they started and are running multi-million dollar corporations, and are admired as leaders. How do they do it?

When it comes to Leadership, which is more important, IQ or EQ or VQ? In which category do you fit?

Should you become more of one or the other, or excel in all three? Why? How?

Without emotion, we feel no conviction to obey the rule of law, experience no environment conducive to logic, and find no reason to check whether a source of facts is credible or corrupt. Emotion is the root of all sales, customer service, coaching, and teaching, parenting, and especially leading.

Every successful advertising campaign is based on emotional photos, music, and well-written copy using colorful adjectives and active verbs. Ninety percent of how people react to anything is based on emotion.

VQ (VALUES QUOTIENT) is the "why" our colleagues and subordinates follow us and allow us to emotionally and intellectually inspire them. Our values are the differentiating factor between a successful leader and a Significant International Leader. Consequently, it is the combination of Intelligence/Knowledge (IQ), Emotion (EQ) and Values (VQ) that prepares us differently to be a Significant International Leader.

- We must go down the organization and reach out to our subordinates to extend our influence, teaching, and mentoring in the spirit that the purpose of a leader is to grow more leaders.
- We must go across the organization, teaching correct principles by example, and inspiring others to govern themselves.
- We must go up the organization to make our leaders look better and be better, because we lead and follow, teach and learn, and act while we are being acted upon, several times every day.

THE SIGNIFICANT WEALTH MODEL is created and sustained through the simultaneous implementation of:

TQ (TRAINING QUOTIENT) is the technical expertise.

MQ (MOTIVATION QUOTIENT) is the passionate desire.

SQ (SERVICE QUOTIENT) is leaving your family, friends, coworkers, community, country and world in better shape than you found them.

SIGNIFICANT WEALTH

Significance

Where TQ, MQ and SQ Interface: Doing Meaningful Things For Others That Make Lots Of Money - Profits Are The Results Of The High Value We Create.

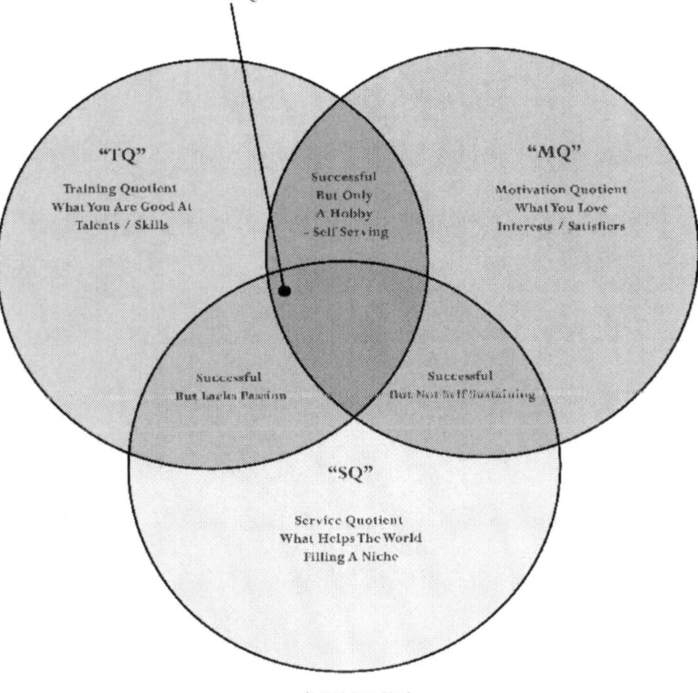

SIGNIFICANT LEADERSHIP

Significance

Where IQ, EQ, and VQ Intersect: Doing Meaningful Things For Others That Are Important.

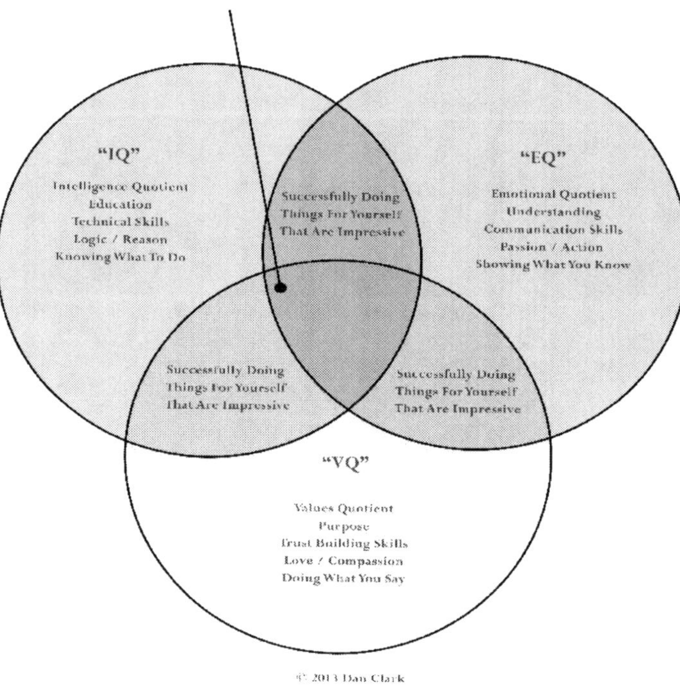

CHAPTER THIRTY-ONE

SIGNIFICANT PARTNER LEADERS ARE SIGNIFICANT HUMAN BEINGS

If you were asked to identify the leaders who have had an incredible influence in your life and the way you approach leadership, who would they be? For me, five stand out above the rest:

Thomas Jefferson: Scholar, Author, Architect, Scientist, Diplomat, Statesman, Founding Father.

American Founding Father Thomas Jefferson was elected to the Virginia House of Burgesses when he was only 25; served in the Continental Congress; was governor of Virginia; a diplomat in France where he helped negotiate the treaties that ended the Revolutionary War; founded the University of Virginia; was fluent in six languages, including Latin, French, Spanish, Italian and Greek, and wrote the Declaration of Independence at the age of 33!

He then served as Secretary of State under George Washington, as Vice President under John Adams; and became the third President of the United States, where he doubled the size of the country by purchasing the Louisiana Territory and then commissioned Lewis and Clark to explore western lands and map the new America.

When you study the life of Jefferson it is clear that he approached leadership from the perspective of a passionate gardener. Jefferson's interest in flowers and planting can be dated to 1766, when he began documenting his naturalistic observations in his Garden Book. As a connoisseur of trees, flowers and gardening techniques the "Gardens of Monticello" were designed and planted by Jefferson on his plantation near Charlottesville, Virginia and included a flower garden, a fruit orchard, and a vegetable garden, which showcased many exotic seeds and plants from his travels abroad.

Out of this love, Jefferson said: "I'm not really a career person. I'm a gardener, basically, who knows we can complain because rose bushes have thorns, or rejoice because thorn bushes have roses. Though an old man, I am but a young gardener. A society grows great when old men plant trees whose shade they know they shall never sit in."

With a focus on service before self and a covenant to leave a legacy of leadership behind Jefferson continued, "Too old to plant trees for my own gratification, I shall do it for my posterity."

It's no wonder then that at a Nobel Prize dinner held at the White House in 1962, President John F. Kennedy greeted his guests: "I think this is the most extraordinary collection of talent, of human knowledge, that has ever been gathered at the White House, with the possible exception of when Thomas Jefferson dined alone."

Clearly, Mr. Jefferson was the consummate Old School Partner Leader who crafted the inspired United States Declaration of Independence that not only inspired each of the Founding Fathers to accept an equal collaborative leadership role that galvanized the original Thirteen Colonies as one country. But, the doctrine proposed in Jefferson's Declaration invited each American citizen to also participate in an experiment in self-governance where 'all men are created equal' and accountable as partners in guaranteeing the inalienable rights to life, liberty and the pursuit of happiness.

Sir Winston Churchill: Statesman, Orator, Peak Performer Under Pressure, War Hero, Legendary Partner Leader.

At the beginning of World War II when the Nazis were conquering the countries throughout Europe and eventually started bombing England in the "Battle of Britain,' it forced Londoners into bomb shelters and the newly elected Prime Minister Winston Churchill to rise to the occasion and fire up his people to stay strong and proud and relentless in their defense of freedom. On two occasions Churchill eloquently put life, liberty and the pursuit of happiness into perfect perspective:

First: "To each there comes in their lifetime a special moment when they are figuratively tapped on the shoulder and offered the chance to do a very special thing, unique to them and fitted to their talents. What a tragedy if that moment finds them unprepared or unqualified for that which could have been their finest hour."

Second: "Never give in, never give in, never, never, never, never - in nothing, great or small, large or petty - never give in except to convictions of honor and good sense... if you will not fight for the right when you can easily win without bloodshed, if you will not fight when your victory will be sure and not too costly, you may come to the moment when you will have to fight with all the odds against you and only a precarious chance of survival. There may be even a worse case. You may have to fight when there is no hope of victory, because it is better to perish than live as slaves."

Clearly, Sir Winston Churchill was the right man at the right time to believe in 'Partner Leadership.' which was the only way to create the coalition of Allied Forces to not only defeat the Nazi's, but to lead the way in the physical reconstruction, financial revitalization and emotional resurgence of war torn Europe.

Barbara Charline Jordan: American Lawyer, Educator, American Civil Rights Leader, Politician, 'Angel of Light and Hope and Dignity For All.' At a tough time in American history during racist segregation, Ms. Jordan rose above it to become the first African American elected to the Texas Senate after Reconstruction, the first Southern African-American woman elected to the United States House of Representatives and the first African-American as well as the first woman to deliver a keynote address at a Democratic National Convention.

Ms. Jordan's work as chair of the U.S. Commission on Immigration Reform, which recommended reducing legal immigration by about one-third, is frequently cited by American 'Immigration Restrictionists.'

Ms. Jordan retired from politics in 1979 and became an adjunct professor teaching ethics at the University of Texas at Austin Lyndon B. Johnson School of Public Affairs. She was again a keynote speaker at the Democratic National Convention in 1992. During her incredible, inspiring, amazing and exemplary life of 'Partner Leadership,' Ms. Jordan received over 20 honorary degrees from institutions across the country, including Harvard and Princeton, received the U.S. Presidential Medal of Freedom and was elected to the Texas and National Women's Halls of Fame. The main terminal at Austin-Bergstrom International Airport is named in her honor where a beautiful statue of Jordan graces its entrance.

Clearly, Barbara Jordan sensed her inherent 'calling' to create a culture of 'Partner Leadership,' which brought together every race, gender, creed and socioeconomic sector who make up America's 'tossed salad' mix of citizens, and advocated for everybody to have access to everything listed in the first paragraph of the Declaration of Independence: *"We hold these truths to be self-evident, that all men (and women) are created equal, that they are endowed by their Creator with certain unalienable Rights, that among these are Life, Liberty and the pursuit of Happiness."*

Muhammad Ali: World Champion, Brave and Bold Communicator, International Ambassador, 'Conscientious' Partner Leader.

In 1988, my hero and three-time World Heavy Weight Boxing Champion Muhammad Ali, invited me as a guest into his home in Berrien Springs, Michigan, and for over four hours taught me four profound truths that immediately intensified my personal courage, and have forever molded my character and desire to be a champion.

For Muhammad Ali, preparation was more than a way of life – it was the way to win. There is a huge difference between training to fight and training to win. Ali ran long distances, did countless sit ups, climbed hills, punched heavy bags and speed bags, jumped rope, and soldiered on practice round after round against stronger and faster sparring partners. At times it had to be mind over body. Most of all, Ali kept at it day after day, month after month, relentlessly dedicated to a grueling routine that was behind that moment in the ring when his opponent was spent and he started dancing.

Boxing was Ali's path to success and significance, self-respect and recognition. At the top of his game in the 'Land of Opportunity' he knew that the playing field wasn't level for all Americans, and boldly challenged the racial status quo to acknowledge his world-class accomplishments, and to respect him as a proud African American man proclaiming, 'I don't have to be what you want me to be!'

In Ali's words, "Impossible is just a big word thrown around by small men who find it easier to live in the world they've been given than to explore the power they have to change it. Impossible is not a fact. It's an opinion. Impossible is not a declaration. It's a dare. Impossible is temporary. Impossible is potential." Possible begins by dreaming the impossible dream.

Clearly, Muhammad Ali understood the significance of 'Partner Leadership' as he used his platform to remind the world that it's important for us to stand for something or we will fall for anything - regardless of race or religion - because the same God who made him, made you and me too!

David Spafford: Billionaire Entrepreneur, Husband, Father, Grandfather, Philanthropist, Spiritual Guide, Fully Alive!

Let me introduce you to a dear friend and mentor of mine, who is one of the smartest and most significant men on planet Earth. David Spafford sustains a perfect blend of obedience to both the cognitive, organizational left side of his brain focused on what's best, and the emotional, relational right side of his brain focused on what's right. With this constant feedback, David can make precise decisions to do right and then persevere in every situation—a skill that has persisted even after David's accession to incredible wealth.

David's path to significance began at age seventeen, when he first decided that he was going to be wealthy. At age nineteen, he became a student of people, purposes, and processes, learning not only from books and schoolteachers, but from a two-year service mission to South Africa undertaken when David was twenty years old. There he became fascinated with men and women running small businesses, tuned into musicians who harmonized their individual notes into synergized symphonies, watched homeless people who still seemed to get what they wanted, and interviewed leaders who had failed so he wouldn't make their same mistakes. When he returned to the States at age twenty-two, David enrolled at the University of Utah and continued to study success principles inside and outside the classroom.

When it came time to start his company, David set up every department and created each job description with a "be brilliant at the basics" attitude. Although he was the visionary who assembled the right people, put them in the right places, and inspired them to greatness, he also trusted enough to stick to what he did best (sales and marketing). He hired others with different strengths to do what he couldn't or didn't want to do.

David established a set of company-wide interpersonal employee rules that created on-the-job harmony and maximized customer satisfaction. The rules provided excellent products, developed and maintained mutually beneficial business relationships, made a profit, grew market shares, made Megahertz a great place to work, and enabled the company to stay the course.

David's obedience and perseverance paid off in a spectacular way. When, at age thirty-four, David sold Megahertz to US Robotics for over $1 billion, not only did he and his two senior executives pocket large sums, but forty employees in his company each put over one million dollars in their pockets. Retired and on top of the world, David and his amazing wife Susan started planning their care-free life of exotic vacations and high adventure hunting and fishing trips—until shocking news came that their two-year-old son Joey was diagnosed with autism. Most couples would feel sorry for themselves and selfishly curse the heavens, crying, "How could you let this happen to me?"

Still living harmoniously, tuning in to their deepest purpose, David and Susan relentlessly sought out the very best doctors and dedicated themselves to giving their precious Joey every opportunity to reach his full potential. They didn't take "no" for an answer but rather accepted their new challenge and responsibility to do whatever it took to help their son. Initially, Joey refused to make eye contact, did not speak, and showed no emotion.

Today, thanks to David's and Susan's tireless adherence to the doc-tor's therapy programs, Joey, now over twenty-one years old, is very engaging and personable. He thrives on eye contact, shares laughter and tears, graduated from the local public high school where he was the most inspirational student on campus, is active in posting on social media, loves to travel, and blesses the lives of all who meet him.

While most of the rich and famous donate money to have buildings named after them selves, David and Susan built and established the Carmen B. Pingree Center for Children with Autism in Salt Lake City, Utah. The Center was named in honor of the woman who helped them in their most critical time of need. They continue to set an ex-ample of how best can and should be right while quietly making everybody around them better and anonymously contributing generous gifts to the charities of their choice so others have a better chance to do right themselves. Living passionately minute to minute has al-lowed David to do the right things simply because they were the right things to do. He believed that regardless of whether he got what he desired, life would still turn out for the best, and he would become better for taking the higher road.

Barry Coburn: Composer, Producer, Esteemed 'Musicon,' Fully Alive!

One individual who understands why and how this songwriting and twelve-note music metaphor works in a practical application way in every aspect of our lives, is the one and only Barry Coburn. Ironically, Barry fully comprehends the significance of living with passion, imagination, and creativity because he is one of the most respected and influential music executives in the world. While the music industry is struggling and failing miserably in so many ways, Barry quietly reminds all of us that in our pursuit of success we are focusing on the wrong thing.

For nearly three decades, Coburn's "Ten Ten Music Group" has been a creative fixture on Nashville's Music Row, and is thriving today. Why?

From the time he entered the music industry at 17 years of age, Barry sensed that the music industry, promoting concerts, and life itself was only about two things: 1) If you get the music right, everything else will fall into place. 2) If you focus all of your time, talent, and resources on helping others become successful, you will become significant in their personal and professional lives. The fame and for-tune will take care of itself. "It's true," Barry says, "you can get any-thing in life that you want if you are willing to help enough other people get what they want."

Barry's philosophy has proven true as he currently has over 13,000 songs in his combined Coburn Music BMI and Ten Ten Music ASCAP catalogs. They feature hit songs written for Taylor Swift, Miley Cyrus, Alan Jackson, Keith Urban, and a theme song in The Chronicles of Narnia.

At age 22, Barry's unique reputation of making it about the music and putting others first, launched a fourteen-year career as the most significant concert promoter in New Zealand and Australia. He worked with the world's biggest acts including Elton John, Led Zeppelin, Black Sabbath, Muddy Waters, and Duke Ellington, while man-aging the mega group Split Enz and blues guitarist Joe Louis Walker.

Barry eventually married and moved to Nashville, Tennessee, where he added artist development and publishing to his promotion and management services. Because everybody likes to do business with a winner, before long Barry was introduced to an unknown Alan Jackson. Although the handsome, charismatic Jackson could sing, it took Barry eighteen months to instill in him the constant passion, imagination, and creativity that was required to become an exceptional songwriter and the true artist he needed to be to make it big and sustain a long significant career.

Because of this, Jackson's first al-bum had four #1s on it. For the twenty-two years that Alan and Barry worked together, Jackson charted thirty-five #1 songs, selling nearly 60 million records during that time.

His music career has now spanned forty years and yet Barry's mission in life has never changed. Every day he wakes up and goes to work, committed to leaving everybody he works with in better shape than he found them – personally and professionally. As the consummate music industry executive, Barry Coburn is one of the last remaining true Artists of Significance!

FOUR 'PARTNER LEADERSHIP' OBSERVATIONS

In an analysis of what these aforementioned influential 'Partner Leaders' have in common, my observations reveal four common understandings:

- Character cannot be developed in ease and quiet. Only through experience of trial and suffering can the soul be strengthened, ambition inspired, and success achieved. Pain either hurts you or helps you change and improve. The difference manifests itself when you understand the difference between the person and the performance. Failure is an event - not a person. Which means stress is not what happens to you. It's your reaction or response to what happens. When we believe things happen 'to' us, we react, which is negative and uncontrolled. When we believe everything happens 'for' us, to build our character and give us experience, we respond, which is positive and something we choose to control.

- If you continue to live in the past, your life will be history. You must create your future from your future. When Edison invented the light bulb, he didn't start by trying to improve the candle. And, while others might think he failed 999 times in his attempt, which would have caused most to quit along the way, Edison rose above his past by looking at the light bulb as an invention with 1000 steps.

- Master martial artist Bruce Lee who said, 'The power of the cup is in its emptiness.' In other words, if the cup is full it has no more room for anything. If we feel we 'have arrived' and have nothing more to learn and no more room to become a better human being, better father, better spouse, manager, leader, coach, worker, neighbor or friend, we are stuck in the drowning waters of diminishing return. What we need to do is fill our cup, then drink it almost dry, and fill it up again, always learning, and as a partner sharing a drink with those who need a drink along the way, only to fill it up again to do it again!

- The un-teachable man is prideful, thinks he knows it all and believes 'what you see is what you get,' with no need to change. Consequently, he is a prisoner in his own mind and body, sentenced to being taught only by his own experiences, which can reach no further than his own pain.

  The teachable man is meek and humble, realizing things don't happen to him, they happen for him, knowing change is nothing more than self-improvement.

Consequently, he is taught by the experiences and pain of others, which reminds him that before he takes action he should make sure the 'juice is worthy of the squeeze.' Then if he fails or falls, at least he failed while attempting to do something noble and right as a partner at home, at work, at school, at play, which keeps him motivated to continuously fill and drink and empty and fill his cup.

CHAPTER THIRTY-TWO

THE 7 PRINCIPLES AND METHODS OF SIGNIFICANT INFLUENCE

1. **PROJECT AUTHORITY (Titles, Ability, Clothing and Presence)**

Titles are powerful symbols of authority and we subconsciously follow them more than the person claiming them. The President of the United States (regardless of his name), Catholic Pope (regardless of his name), Pastor, The Most Reverend, Your Majesty The King/Queen, His Excellency, General, Admiral, Commander, Chief Master Sergeant, Dad, Mom, Grand Father, Grand Mother, Teacher, Coach, Teammate, Mentor, Principal, Officer Of The Law, Your Honor The Judge, Brother, Sister, Neighbor, Friend.

For example, I was in Baghdad, Iraq, at Ballad Base and the Base Commander was a Colonel in the U.S. Air Force. He was an amazing human being, a brave and heroic warrior, and an exceptional leader. But because he was not a General Officer, he got little respect from his Army counter-parts who were Generals.

As soon as he got his promotion to One Star Brigadier General, although he didn't get any more authority, responsibility or power, didn't change his management style, didn't learn more, or suddenly become a better leader, because his title was higher and more respected, he became an instant member of the "Generals Brotherhood" that warranted him instant respect as an equal.

Another kind of authority symbol that triggers our subconscious compliance is clothing. Our uniforms talk way before we do. A police officer's uniform gets us to check our speedometer, feel in trouble (if we should) and feel safe and secure if we need to. His uniform, not the person wearing the uniform, gives him the right to stand in the road, direct the traffic of total strangers, and arrest a bank robber or intervene in domestic violence.

The referee in many sporting events wears a striped shirt that guarantees whatever he says goes. If you argue with his decision, you will pay the consequences of ejection.

In human interaction, authoritative qualities and actions include tone of voice, (lower voices are more authoritative), the loudness of your voice (those using a microphone are perceived to have authority and be in control), the height of your stature (when speaking to a group you gain instant credibility and respect if you are raised on a stage above them), and your self-image (confidence to project as one having authority).

We also know health is extremely important to all of us. Therefore, physicians hold the position of respected authorities in a defined power and prestige structure, where no one can ever override a physician's decision in a case. Automatically obeying the doctor's orders has become the rule in every culture.

In 2010, the only two players on the NFL Indianapolis Colts football team who were eating Power Bars before each game were non-starting linemen. Nobody cared or paid attention to them. But as soon as their star quarterback, Peyton Manning, decided to also eat the energy boosting bars, everybody started eating them.

Because of his exceptional ability, his teammates watched everything he did, and believed that if they thought, ate and worked out exactly like Peyton did, they too could excel at their positions. At the time Peyton was traded to the Denver Broncos no one was eating Power Bars before a game. Suddenly the entire team did. And the one time Peyton ate three bars before a game, each team member also ate three bars before that game!

What job "Title" would give you more credibility at work? What do you have to do (additional training, more experience), in order to obtain this title?

What one new "Ability" and improved level of performance could you acquire that would immediately attract a higher level of admiration from your peers, and inspire them to duplicate your eating, exercise, and preparation habits?

What one thing can you improve in your wardrobe selection (having both your professional and personal shirts laundered, starched and pressed, polishing your shoes and boots, etc.), and/or "tweak" on your uniform that will increase the level of class, sophistication, and polished image you project as a leader?

2. ASK THE RIGHT QUESTIONS

If you think about it, you cannot, not answer a question. Questions create immediate involvement. Out of the Nine Influencers in your toolbox, our ability to question is the most often used by master persuaders. Skilled negotiators ask more than twice as many questions as average negotiators. Questions elicit an automatic response from our brains. Even if we don't verbalize the answer, we think of a response every time we are asked a question. For this reason, life is not about answers; it's about questions. To illustrate:

A college professor asked his students to list what they thought were the Seven Wonders of the World. Out of the one hundred students in the lecture hall, the general consensus was:

Egypt's Pyramid of Giza
Great Wall of China
Petra of Jordan
Taj Mahal
Stonehenge
Machu Picchu
Roman Coliseum

While gathering the votes, the professor noted that one young woman had not yet finished her paper. He asked if she was having trouble answering the question. She replied, "No, I'm not having trouble with the answer, I'm having trouble with the question. Why only seven? According to who and what criteria? What does 'wonder' mean to you, and is it different for me?"

The professor responded, "Tell us what you have, and maybe we can help." The young woman hesitated, and then read: "I think the real Seven Wonders of the World are: To Think, to See, to Hear, to Taste, to Touch, to Laugh, and to Love."

The room was so quiet you could have heard a pin drop. The professor took a deep breath and replied, "Wow! This is the most profound lesson we will learn all year. And isn't it pathetic that out of the 101 people in this room - me included - that only one of us, only one percent, understands that the things we overlook as simple and fundamental truly are wondrous."

This story provides three powerful reminders:

- The most significant and precious things in life cannot be bought or built by hand.
- Before we look for answers outside of ourselves, let us first look within.
- Life is not about answers; it's about questions.

He or she who asks the questions is in complete control of the conversation.

You can get wrong answers from negative questions and you can get wrong answers from right questions, but you cannot get right answers from the wrong questions. Only when we ask the right questions can we get the right answers and progress to the next right question.

Right answers are not always the solution. Right answers don't necessarily solve the problem. For example, consider the answer "Don't Drink and Drive." It's right, yet many people still drive drunk. Only right questions solve problems.

To produce a more specific answer from those under the influence, we must ask a more specific question. "Why must you drive right now?" Followed by, "Is there another way or form of transportation?" Which, if nothing else, produces a better answer:

"Because I have not been drinking, I will help you get to where you are going safely."

Questions beginning with "why" and "who" are more emotionally charged than "what" or "how" questions because "why" and "who" questions are historical in nature. They take us back in time. "Why did this happen?" "Why must you drive drunk now?" "Who messed up?" They plead for reasons, but they breed excuses. We all despise excuses and get annoyed when others use them on us, but the fault is usually with the one asking the wrong "why/who" questions. They are simply answering the question we asked.

Instead of asking people to live in the past, we should ask future-oriented questions like, "How can we fix this?" or "What can we do right now to stop the decline and turn this around?" These inquiries invite people to live in the present, encouraging positive statements about how things can be done better in the future. These questions are not about how to be a different person, but about how to become more of who and what we already are.

Pick a topic. Visualize interviewing a person about this topic. Write a "why" question and a "who" question. Now change your mindset from only seeking information to inspiring the person to improve his/ her performance and write a "what" question and a "how" question.

3. EXEMPLIFY ABUNDANCE

Having a scarcity mentality is extremely negative and counter-productive. If we believe success is limited, that there is only "just enough for me" and therefore, I will scratch, kick and claw my way to the top, cheat, steal, step on and over others, and burn bridges to get the small amount of success that is available at the moment, we may have short term results, but in the long haul, we will fail miserably.

These are they who have stopped dreaming mighty dreams, risking and growing and working hard on a good, clean, pure, powerful, positive goal; those who are stagnant and out of insecurity, put others down to make themselves feel like they are progressing and better than they are. We must never have a scarcity mentality. We must have an Abundance Mentality.

The primary purpose in life is to make ourselves better today than we were yesterday, so we are in the required positive emotional state to make everybody else around us better to the degree they say, "I like me best when I'm with you I want to see you again."

We must understand that we are sharing this world with all living creatures. The only way we will ever avert war, establish world peace, stop global warming, eliminate hunger, cure disease, defeat poverty and create a world in which everybody believes they are here for a reason, is to believe that the same God who made you made me too, and to have an Abundance Mentality toward influence that no matter who you are or where you live, there is enough to go around for all of us!

4. SHOW RESPECT

Letting someone down is when we feel the most guilt and remorse. Fear motivation, "you do it or else," has always been ineffective in increasing performance, even in the military when following orders is mandatory, because it only works when authority is there to hold us accountable. Being a champion is determined by what we do when authority is NOT around. It's what we do when the manager, coach, parent, teacher, officer, NCO is not watching that makes us or breaks us. The only fear motivation that works, is not being afraid of the consequences of breaking the rules and getting caught, but rather, being afraid of letting your employer, coach, teacher or parent down. This is called Respect and it is out of respect for the law, for others, for our family name, and for ourselves, that we do the right thing simply because it is the right thing to do.

5. CREATE A CONDUCIVE ATMOSPHERE

Atmosphere is merely a state of mind you create and control. Whether you're in a Shopping Mall, Casino, Sports Bar, Exclusive Dance Club, Amusement Park or Theme Restaurant, when you walk in, each establishment purposefully evokes a specific calculated atmosphere and feeling. The old popular television series, "Cheers," was entirely built around the premise of a bar with an atmosphere where they "know your name."

Lighting, interior design and décor are the obvious creators of atmosphere. And let us not forget location, location, location as far as projecting class and a "safe neighborhood." Additionally, there is cost of en-try and price of products and services, which portrays sophistication, and an elite sense of Scarcity and Social Proof. But even more powerful than these outward creators of atmosphere, are the not so obvious subtleties of music and aroma.

Aroma is commonly used as a participation device that evokes memories faster than any other influence. Car dealers depend on the New Car Smell, even in their Used Cars to increase image, which translates to a higher asking price and easier sale. Victoria Secret uses potpourri scents to stimulate customer's feelings and sense of femininity.

"Cinnabon" bakes their fresh cinnamon rolls in their small kiosk. Asthe distinct aroma seeps into the large atmosphere of the Mall or airport concourse, the smell suddenly stimulates the need in those passing by to satisfy a craving they did not previously have for a hot, fresh, generously frosted, lip smacking, and decadent cinnamon roll delight!

I read where Japan's Kajima Corporation has taken the influence of atmosphere to the point where they use the specific aromas of citrus in the A.M. for its arousing effects, floral scents at midday to increase concentration, and forest/woodland scents in the P.M. at the end of the work day to relax their employees before they head home to their families. The management at Kajima is convinced that aroma literally increases and sustains productivity throughout the day.

Let us not forget the different atmospheres in each stadium of the National Football League. I attended a game in Charlotte, North Carolina, at the Carolina Panthers stadium where the pre-game was family-oriented with a carnival atmosphere filled with food kiosks, throwing and catching games for both children and their parents to play, face painting for the children, fairly conservatively dressed cheerleaders (compared to all the others in the league) who were accessible, interacting with the fans, taking photos and signing autographs.

The entire parking lot area outside the stadium, all the way to the cheapest seats inside the stadium, felt safe and secure. They respected the opposing teams fans who had come to watch the game and only talked trash in a fun rivalry way.

The entire game I never heard one "F-Bomb" dropped and no fights broke out in the stands. Everybody was dressed in bright happy colors with a general sense of style, sophistication and class. If I lived in Charlotte I would take my entire family to every game and regardless of the price of admission, be season ticket holders.

Three weeks later I attended an Oakland Raiders game in their home stadium in Alameda, California. The famous "Black Hole" is the nickname for the section of fanatical fans who are the loudest and most abusive and is a real deal. The visiting team bus must drive through it to enter the stadium and visitors' locker room. At any home game it is common place to see an elderly grand-mother holding the hand of her eight-year-old granddaughter, both wearing black and silver Raiders jerseys with their faces painted, standing on the roadside flipping the bird to the opposing team as they enter "Raider Nation."

From the moment I got out of my car I thought I could be mugged at any turn. I am 6' 5" 240 lbs. and used to play ball and I was nervous the entire day! "F-Bombs" every couple of sentences, everybody walking around dressed in black, tattooed out, thinking they were the "baddest boys in the hood." I saw three fights picked with people who were wearing the other team's jerseys!

The cheerleaders were not accessible and the atmosphere in the parking lot and especially in certain sections of the stadium was one of hard core, gang banging, Hell's Angels intimidation. Not a great atmosphere for children and consequently, there were few families in attendance.

6. EMOTIONALLY STIR WITH MUSIC

Music is a major part of Atmosphere. Department Store surveys prove that shoppers who are exposed to music make 17 percent more purchases and shop 18 percent longer than shoppers in stores not playing music. There are even styles, rhythms and pitches of music that effect shoppers in specific ways. Fast food restaurants need up-tempos, while grocery shoppers respond best to slow tempos. Music changes our mood and internal energy flow. It mellows us when we are hyper, calms us when we are nervous, and fires us up when we are down and out.

Music changes our behavior. It's like the woman driving in front of you on the freeway who is listening to "ABBA" on the radio, putting along at 25 miles an hour, her overcoat stuck in the door, the belt dangling on the road. She's had her left hand turn signal on for the last fifty miles, totally oblivious to the fast moving real world around her because she is singing, "You are the dancing queen, young and sweet, only seventeen." Then, at its conclusion, she turns her radio to a rock station where Guns N' Roses is screaming, "Welcome to the Jungle," influencing her to accelerate up to 90 miles an hour in a school zone with kids diving into the bushes to get out of the way!

It's a proven fact that we can change attitudes and actually improve performance at work by playing the right music that creates the right ambiance, depending on the mood required by that department.

To be most effective, music should create an atmospheric presence that employees and customers are not consciously aware of until they no longer hear it. When they suddenly feel differently, they tie that emptiness into being away from you, your organization, or out of your store/club/restaurant and want to come back to feel it and hear it some more!

7. AGREE ON AN INSPIRING "WHY" WITH COMPLETE TRAINING AND SUPPORT

The previous Six Principles and Methods of Influence are obviously focused on persuading prospects to become external customers and clients of our organizations and enterprises. #7 focuses on influencing our internal customers and employees/subordinates to become more of who they already are - everything they have the potential to be. We cannot influence others to increase their performance and maximize individual productivity unless they get five things from us, their leaders:

Inspiring self-motivation to the point they make winning personal, by fully understanding "what" you are asking, and "why" he/she is doing it. Because Influencing another is a process, it begins when the leader and the subordinate reach an equal agreement, with the same level of passion and commitment dedicated to accomplishing the designated task and achieving the desired outcome.

When we are baffled by the fact that others won't do what they know they should do, we must ask, "Can they do it?" Motivation without education and training breed's frustration. Before our subordinates can be expected to accomplish a task they have never done before you, their leader, must first recognize their talent (which reveals to themselves a genuine interest in tackling the task, which in turn stirs personal motivation), and then provide the required knowledge and skill development necessary to enact each and every behavior.

Because it's what we do when the leader/ manager/coach is not around that illuminates our integrity, commitment to excellence, and work ethic, once we have inspired and properly trained our subordinates, we must put in place the proper "positive peer pressure" support system required to keep their personal motivation alive. Unless our colleagues value our attitude and behavior, it's only a matter of time before we slip back into the same old behavior we were in before the leader attempted to improve it.

Once we initiate personal motivation, train, and establish the emotional support system for those we are influencing, it is critical that we now surround them with highly motivated, equally trained, equally skilled and technically proficient coworkers who will help them change, grow, improve, and succeed in doing that which is necessary.

Because achieving our desired results are often thrown off course by people, places and things outside of our control, sometimes morphing into different results than originally sought, it is imperative that we continuously reward the process of improvement and recognize our people for their efforts along the way. Incentivizing the journey is the structural requirement that allows the previously mentioned six Principles and Methods to work!

CHAPTER THIRTY-THREE

'BEST' LEADERS FAIL

'RIGHT' LEADERS SUCCEED AND BECOME SIGNIFICANT PARTNERS

I've always believed leaders succeed because of six words: Vision, Backbone, Integrity, Model and Hubris. Although most of our reference to human chemistry is usually about sports teams, CEOs, politicians, and military leaders have the same impact on their teams as do coaches.

Legendary corporate leaders such as Lee Iacocca when he was at Ford Motor Company and later as the CEO of Chrysler Corporation; Jack Welch, CEO of GE; Bill Gates of Microsoft; and Steven Jobs who started Apple Computers, were personally responsible for creating the correct formula for sharing the vision, setting the course, generating the energy, directing the recruiting and hiring of the right employees, and maintaining the morale necessary to create their companies into the winning teams they were and still are today.

Powerful government leaders such as George Washington, Thomas Jefferson, Abraham Lincoln, John F. Kennedy, Ronald Reagan, Winston Churchill, Mahatma Gandhi, and the father and founder and first president of the United Arab Emirates, His Excellency Sheik Zayed bin Sultan Al Nahayan, were the main and most important characters in the organization of their countries and in establishing freedom, fairness, and prosperity in their regions of the world.

Legendary military leaders such as World War II British General Sir Bernard Montgomery, American generals Douglas MacArthur, George Patton, and Desert Storm Norman Schwarzkopf, were responsible for the planning and winning of certain battles and ending major wars.

VISION

Some want to call their leadership ability "charisma" and they definitely had that. But Charisma can be as much a liability as an asset, as one of the most damaging trends in the corporate world is a board of directors selecting a dazzling, celebrity, egocentric, attention-seeking person to call their leader. The reason any leader is successful is not because of their "piercing eyes and sexy smile." It's because they are people-centric, service-centric, success-seeking individuals who live lives of Significance because of their long-term vision. This is what makes them exciting to be around and easy to follow!

Anyone who has studied the lives and management styles of the aforementioned leaders will conclude that, yes, they became celebrity leaders as the world knows their names, but it was not because of their magnetic personality. It was because they had Vision and could help others see it, feel it, and fully embrace it together in the same cause of achieving greatness.

BACKBONE

Vaclav Havel wrote, "Vision is not enough. It must be combined with venture. It is not enough to stare up the steps, we must step up the stairs." Which means that Significant Partner Leaders also have a character-based backbone – strong and straight so they are able to stand for something and stay true to their core values. They have a wishbone – dreaming big with the firm conviction that all things are possible if they just conceive, believe, and do that which is necessary to achieve. And, they have a funny bone – making following them, working and/or playing for them fun.

Because they know failure is an event, not a person, they always take what they are doing extremely serious, but only while they maintain a sense of humor based on humility that allows them to take their title and themselves with a grain of salt.

INTEGRITY

Significant Partner Leaders also succeed because of another word: Integrity. Two classic examples come from the great state of Colorado. Two-term Republican Governor Bill Owens was elected with a Republican majority in both the House and Senate. Two issues on the ballot, stronger restrictions on abortion and school vouchers, were voted down 2 to 1 by the voters. These were both strong conservative issues and two days after the election all the Republican lawmakers said "oh good, we can now pass these laws the way we choose."

Governor Owens said, "Absolutely not. The people of Colorado have spoken and have voted against both of these issues. I respect that. End of discussion. These are now non issues and don't bring them up again."

As Governor Owens was finishing his service, the six-year District Attorney for the city of Denver and lifelong Democrat Bill Ritter decided to run. The Democratic Party told him he had to change his stance on two issues and become more mainstream in order to get their endorsement. But being a devout Catholic he said "no, this is what I have always believed and surely you don't expect me to change my convictions for you or to just get elected," and he never wavered.

Bill stuck to his guns and publicly stated he was against abortion and gay marriage. The Democratic Party tried desperately to run three different opponents against him in the primaries but they failed and he got the nomination. Because of his integrity, Bill Ritter won a landslide election by 17 points getting both republicans and democrats to vote for him.

MODEL

Significant Partner Leaders are the 'right' leaders because they subscribe to a time-tested system in which they operate and build their culture. One of the most well-known leadership formulas that quickly turns Followers and Admirers into Leaders, which then can grow fellow leaders into Passionate Partners is called the "COG's" Ladder Model, which is made up of Seven Building Blocks:

- Clear Objectives. A group must have a reason for being together defined by group goals.
- Openness. Everybody must contribute their ideas, opinions, and experience with confidence.
- Trust and Support. Honest communication breeds trust.
- Cooperation through Conflict. If two people agree on everything it means one of them is not necessary.
- Competence. You can have the most perfectly balanced, well-oiled, high-spirited group in the world, but if there is no one in the group with the knowledge, technical skills, and competence required for the task at hand, there is little chance that a team can form or the mission can be accomplished.
- Individual Development. Good teams push their members and challenge them to improve themselves and become all they can be, so they can in turn contribute more to the benefit of making the team all it can be.
- Leadership. Whether formal or informal, as leaders do not require a title, someone rises above of the rest to motivate the others and bind the group together.

HUBRIS

Significant Partner Leaders understand the short and long term consequences of succumbing to one word: 'Hubris' – "The inerrant belief that I am right; that I know more than everybody else and therefore I don't have to be accountable to anybody." In the last few years the list of well-known leaders who have failed is mind-boggling. U.S. President Bill Clinton was one of our better presidents with his deficit reduction, welfare reform, minimum wage increase, and of course the Oslo Accord. Then he got tangled up with Miss Monica, in the sacred and historic surroundings of the Oval Office, lied under oath, and was impeached.

In 2006, Ted Haggerty, head of the New Life Christian Church – a 14,000-member church in Colorado Springs, Colorado and president of the multi-million-member American Evangelical Association, preached from his pulpit every Sunday against gay marriage. Three days before the 2006 election deciding a gay rights amendment, he was exposed for having a homosexual relationship with a gay prostitute for the last three years and doing drugs (methamphetamine) while having sex.

Bernie Ebbers, president/CEO of MCI/World Com, who had built the largest communications company in the world, manufactured false earnings by inflating revenues and shoving costs to the future to increase stock prices. Auditors exposed him and now he is spending the rest of his life in prison.

Enron's president/CEO Ken Lay did the same thing as Ebbers, was also convicted and sentenced to life in prison and died shortly thereafter. William McGuire, president of United Healthcare, had 700 mil-lion dollars in stock and got caught back-dating other stock options to generate another 300 million dollars to secretly and illegally put in his pocket. What? 700 million wasn't enough?

And let us not forget Bernie Madoff who was arrested in December of 2008 for orchestrating the $50 billion-dollar heist of the century. For years Madoff and his company Bernard Madoff Investment Securities LLC "BMIS," perpetrated fraud on their powerful, sophisticated and wealthy clients in a massive "Ponzi" pyramid scheme.

They paid double-digit returns out of funds sent to Madoff by new investors, rather than from existing client's actual returns on their in-vestments. Larger than the Enron losses, this "kiting" scam ravaged family trusts, New York and West Palm Beach based charitable institutions, and huge hedge funds.

The saddest and scariest part in these horrific examples is that each of these immoral shysters knew they were doing wrong and yet consciously and will-fully broke the law and "sinned" with no remorse except that they got caught!

CHAPTER THIRTY-FOUR

THE TWO-PART SYSTEM FOR CREATING A SIGNIFICANT PARTNER LEADERSHIP CULTURE

"Once you get the culture right
the rest of the stuff takes care of itself."
– Peter Drucker

This two-part system illuminates the quotes listed at the end of Chapter One that describe the 'Rock Bottom' mindset required to create a Culture of Significant Partner Leadership. Of all the requirements facing leaders today, the key question is how do we get people from different philosophies, political views, job descriptions, and levels of authority to follow us and respond to our requests? The answer lies in an understanding of a System made up of Nine Elements divided into Two Parts:

(PART ONE)

Part One focuses on creating and sustaining Loyalty, Optimistic Flexible Adjustments and Momentum.

LOYALTY

The way you treat your staff will be mirrored in your customer relationships. Inspiring and maintaining player/employee loyalty is most critical because customer turnover and employee turnover are directly related. Customers are oftentimes more loyal to the employee than they are to the brand. For this reason, we must ensure that the employees believe they are a major part of the brand.

I used to believe employee loyalty was bought and paid for with salaries, raises, bonuses and benefits. I was dead wrong. Loyalty is as intimate as loving and can never be forced. Just as the Bonnie Raitt song says, "I can't make you love me anymore," so it is with loyalty. Champion owners, leaders, and managers know that getting and keeping "right" players/employees is the secret to attracting and keeping right and loyal customers for the company. In order to create and maintain the loyalty, players/employees need to fully understand the eight component parts of maintaining employee loyalty. Incidentally, these eight suggestions also work in churches and synagogues to maintain their member activity and in the military to retain their best people:

CREATING AND MAINTAINING LOYALTY

- We must always base our self-respect and respect for others on brutal honesty with no sucking up or brownnosing. We, and the players/ employees must be 100 percent honest with ourselves in order to be totally honest with others, and to be implicitly trusted by every sub-ordinate who reports to us.
- We must always give proper and complete training before we give employees a new task, providing equal authority with the responsibility. Employees must be able to make necessary decisions required to do their assignments when leadership and management are not around.
- We must always treat employees like social beings. Employees have lives outside of work - sick kids, aging parents, school programs to attend, and concerts and games to support on weekends. They go to church and

are involved in politics and service organizations. Subordinates must be allowed to balance their lives. Supervisors must be flexible — both task- and relationship-oriented, not merely time-oriented. Supervisors should do special things for their employees' children, spouses, and significant others. Off-task time is the place to increase and strengthens on-task performance.

- We must make sure all employees firmly believe that they work for "their" company. If you do the first three, number 4 will take care of itself!
- We must make sure that all players/employees have complete knowledge of products, policies, procedures, goals, and so forth. They must understand and fully comprehend what the company or organization does.
- We must make sure all employees have a deep conviction that what the company or organization does is good, positive, and right.
- We must make sure each employee has a friend at work. Whenever people start a new job (or change churches, synagogues, neighborhoods, schools, etc.), they usually leave associates, friends, social life, and a support system behind. Without making an immediate social transition by making new friends at the job, employees return to old friends and associates.
- They may also resort to old habits and behaviors that don't fit into the new work culture. If they feel out of place at work, they may at first stay away emotionally. That may be followed by inactivity, absence, and finally, dismissal or resignation.
- We must make sure every employee has an opportunity to serve. The service must be more than a project—it needs to become a way of life. Service changes who we are!

OPTIMISTIC FLEXIBLE ADJUSTMENTS
"DON'T WASTE A GOOD RECESSION!"

Leadership is not a step-by- step program list of things to do, but rather a condition of the heart. Leaders don't seek to control, they liberate. The fruits of an exceptional leader appear predominantly among the followers. Are the subordinates reaching their full potential? Are they learning and serving? Do the followers understand and accept diversity? Can they manage conflict? In 2008 through 2010, did they understand that they should Never Waste A Good Recession?

The only the organizations which survived and thrived during the brutal global economic down turn were those who had leaders with finely tuned "Partner Leadership Skills," who believed and executed the following seven psychologies in a passionate, positive plan of action:

They acknowledged there really is a global recession – things are bad. They realized their customers and co-workers really were hurting. If you sugarcoat this you lose credibility. True leaders and man-agers accept and acknowledge that this current world economy has caused a lot of fear and pain. Partner Leadership is aligning your emotions and empathetic understanding with the stress, pain and emotions of those whom you lead and the customers you serve.

We've had energy induced recessions (in the '70s gas prices went sky-high with long lines at the pumps). We've had credit induced recessions (in the late '80s and early '90s with the S&L failures, banks stopped lending until a huge government bailout). We've had housing induced recessions (from 1983 to 1993 homes lost value and traded down). But this is the first recession in my lifetime where all three of these causes created and continue to fuel a recession all at the same time!

Clearly, it was the organizations who invested in their people that survived and thrived during the recession. While their competitors laid off extraordinary, talented, highly skilled and experienced man-agers and sales professionals, these visionary, significant companies took advantage of this leadership windfall and hired them and trained them in their culture, products and services.

When the recession ended these companies were stronger, more deeply embedded in their communities, and owned more of the market share because:

- In a recessionary environment everybody must be a "Producer." It's all hands on deck! It's do whatever it takes to live to fight another day! It's now we fully understand what it means to be part of a Partner Leadership culture where it's "our company and our challenge and our destiny and only when everybody wins can I win."
- They invested in innovation. While most companies went on "survival mode," and eliminated research and development, they knew that it takes 1 to 3 years to bring a new product to market. Therefore, they invested, invented, developed, produced and tested new state-of-the-art technology and products so as soon as the recession showed signs of ending they were rolled out and sold. (Apple is the #1 example of this as they introduced new iPod applications and iPad innovation during 2009 and 2010.)
- They adjusted their measurement metric of success and changed the way they kept score and compensated for sales and productivity. They reset realistic goals with manageable expectations so the employees could keep themselves motivated, knowing success breeds success.
- They didn't isolate themselves and didn't hide. If a wolf knocked at their door, they invited him in and made a fur coat! Their leaders embraced all of their employees, especially their sales force. In down markets, it is the time to position ourselves and establish our value, show our strengths and gain respect!
- They cut costs, got lean and mean, eliminated wasted time, minimized processes and paper work, downsized "luxury jobs," right-sized administrative assistants, and

flattened the organizational chart to no more than three "direct reports."

- Those companies that did not survive the global recession only cut their costs and shrunk the size of the pie. Those who thrived enlarged the pie!

MOMENTUM

From this list I trust it is obvious that the most important assignment any leader has is to create and maintain momentum. Leaders can delegate efficiency (doing things right), but they can never delegate effectiveness (doing the right things). They must deal personally with effectiveness to do whatever is necessary to keep the momentum alive.

Momentum is lost when leaders allow the organization to become something it is not; when they start confusing activity with accomplishment; when they begin to confuse celebrities with real heroes; when problem causers begin to outnumber problem curers; when customers are considered interruptions instead of opportunities; and when the highest ranking executives confuse pleasure with meaning, causing superficial communication among other leaders and/or with subordinates.

CHAPTER THIRTY-FIVE

THE TWO-PART SYSTEM FOR CREATING A SIGNIFICANT PARTNER LEADERSHIP CULTURE

(PART TWO)

Right leaders simply do the right thing, simply because it's the right thing to do. Doing right comes from knowing what's right, so Part Two focuses on Goals, Objectives, Delegation, Responsibility, Setting Expectations and Eliminating Unrealistic Expectations.

SETTING GOALS AND OBJECTIVES

Although goals and objectives are different, the one thing they share in common is that people who don't set them and work toward achieving them either live in their past because they have nothing going on in their present, or because they are stuck and stagnate, they put others down to make themselves feel like they are moving forward.

Because life is what happens while we are making other plans, the only way we can take charge of our lives is to perfect the art of setting goals and objectives, and to know the difference. "Old school" says to set short-term and long-term goals with no mention of objectives.

"My school" says goals are only an excuse for the game. We play the game in between the goals. If the only satisfaction you get is at the final destination, you will miss the joy in the journey and will spend your life merely hoping to be happy.

There is a distinct difference between goals and objectives. Goals are short-term, and both the activity and the outcome must be controlled 100 percent by us. Objectives constitute everything else that involves people, weather, transportation, and so forth that we cannot control. Winning the game or championship is not a goal—there are too many variables. It is an objective.

Coming early to work and staying late if needs be, driving three hours to deliver extraordinary customer service and create customer delight, playing each play one at a time, blocking this guy, tackling that ball carrier, lifting weights today, pushing myself to run faster and longer tomorrow, studying more film than any other teammate, practicing, and focusing on giving it everything I have when less would be sufficient, all constitute goals.

Relying on somebody else to close my sale, take me to work, exe-cute the block or tackle, spot me in the weight room, drive me to practice, or fly me to the game—these things are objectives. What makes our personal goal setting exciting and ultimately rewarding is when it helps the large organization or team achieve the team objective. Success comes when we relentlessly work toward achieving short-term controllable personal goals. Success stays as we passionately share our long-term organizational objectives and agree to pursue them as a unified team.

Most people buy into this explanation until the goals and/or objectives seem unreasonable. When this occurs whining, moaning, complaining, and backbiting usually accompany the so-called expectations and productivity goes down instead of up. To combat this we need to get others to buy into our goals and objectives so we can solicit their influence and support to get others on board to accomplish the required organizational outcomes and desired results. This is called Delegation.

DELEGATION

After we set clear goals and objectives, which clarifies our long-term vision and short-term needs, it is time to perfect the art and process of "delegation." The very nature of the quoted belief, "You can do any-thing but you can't do everything," implies that we should do what we are suited for, let others do the same and together we are more. The one in charge decides who does what and delegates the teamwork assignments.

According to Webster, delegation is "To assign responsibility; to send or appoint one to represent another." When it comes to delegation, regardless of what the leader, manager, coach may or may not be saying and doing, the perception to the players, employees and subordinates is that "the insensitive, inconsiderate boss is giving me more work and another assignment so he can free up his own time and balance out his work/family life."

Unless this perception and/or reality is circumvented and changed by the one in charge, all direction and encouragement pertaining to objectives, goals and winning will never come to fruition. If the boss says, "do more with less," and isn't willing to practice what he preaches and more importantly preach only what he practices, the seed of resentment is planted and the fruits of confusing activity with accomplishment start to appear.

We must remember that it's what we do when the leader/manager/coach is not around that determines the success or failure of the team, and when there is resentment between boss and worker, the worker will only work when the boss is watching.

The central doctrine of delegation is based on the knowledge that leaders don't tell people what to do and definitely don't ask them to do something they are not willing to do themselves. Instead, you share the vision and clarify the cause, present the opportunity, inspire them to take ownership, and then lead by example through full participation so that your collective efforts ease the burden of each team member individually.

In an interesting part of the U.S. military culture, I have noticed that the highest-ranking person in the mess hall always waits to be served last to ensure that all of his airmen get something to eat.

When it comes time for any of these leaders to ask his/her subordinates to "bear one another's burdens," because mutual respect and support is already in place and practiced daily, the so-called delegation is perceived as nothing more than "all for one and one for all – when the water in the lake goes up, all the boats rise together."

RESPONSIBILITY

Understanding the word responsibility is always good. The first half of the word – Response, means "taking best appropriate action to a thought or situation." By nature, however, it is still a reaction and fluctuates between "will you" or "won't you." The second part of Responsibility - Ability, never fluctuates because it's always about if you "can" or "can't." And if you can, you must lead, give more, serve more, do more, and be more.

Take it to the ultimate level, consistently win and get what you want – not just because, "where much is given, much is expected," and it's expected by others, but because it's demanded of yourself.

Responsibility is recognizing the relationship between pain and gain, payment and prize. We all have heard, "No pain no gain." We have to pay the price every day in order to enjoy the prize forever. Responsibility is making the right choice based on that recognition, and then living with the choice without concern. Therefore, taking responsibility for being and doing right is the key to success in every aspect of our lives.

We must go deeper than the peripheral understanding of society's claim that leaders are responsible, period – that the buck must stop somewhere and it is ultimately at the top. Yes and no, but only when you completely realize that the coach/leader/manager is only responsible to people, not for them. We cannot improve others; rather, we can only inspire them to change their minds, objectives, and goals, so their way to proceed, vision, and clarity of cause and reason to improve is as clear as ours.

For example, in relationships, love is not the answer - it's the assignment. In business, customer service is not the answer - it's the assignment. As we all know, customer service is not a department—it's an attitude. Customer service and sales are everybody's business! It doesn't matter if we are corporate executives, first-year employees, professionals, teachers, coaches, or parents. We all meet at the same place—at the customer.

At Nordstrom department stores, achieving success is simple. Nordstrom's has only one rule: "Take care of the customer, and use your best judgment." Their "you can return your purchase without question" policy revolutionized customer service practices of the day.

In their shoe department, they constantly reinforce this message by training the sales staff to always measure both feet, because most people have one foot that is slightly larger than the other. This drastically reduces the number of shoe returns as most are caused by poor comfort and fit.

If Nordstrom's had a long list of rules, the employee would say there is too much to deal with and would become frustrated. Frustrated workers become indifferent to the customer, focusing too much attention on the system and not enough on the customer, who needs to feel wanted and important.

Yes, we leaders are responsible to others, not for others. Therefore, we must constantly remind those whom we lead that they cannot merely think their way to a new way of living. They must live their way to a new way of thinking. This obviously applies to ourselves, as all outcomes in our existence will be determined by the values, attributes, and traits we choose to live by.

Discovering this insight into the psychology of a leader is sometimes difficult, frustrating, and frightening. After four thousand years of recorded history, the two most difficult things we have to deal with are failure and success—both of which are internal issues we are responsible for.

SETTING SIGNIFICANT EXPECTATIONS

Internal expectations begin and end with self-respect. Whitney Griswold, President of Yale University said, "Self-respect cannot be hunted or purchased. It is never for sale. It cannot be fabricated out of public relations. It comes to us when we are alone, in quiet moments, in quiet places, when we suddenly realize that, knowing the good, we have done it; knowing the beautiful, we have served it; knowing the truth, we have spoken it."

Out of self- respect, we don't wait for failure to kick-start self-improvement. We don't wait for sickness to kick-start our healthy eating and exercise program. We definitely don't let a negative thing that someone else says or does change the positive person we are. Out of respect for ourselves we always think and do something to become better today than we were yesterday - physically, mentally, spiritually, emotionally, financially, socially, and to make our families stronger.

We do it, not because it is expected by others, but because it is demanded of ourselves. Not competing against others, but only to inspire us and motivate us to work harder to reach our ultimate capacity and potential as a human being and become more of who we already are.

As an illustration of expectations, let us use personal relationships and marriage. Currently there is a 50 percent divorce rate in America. Why? Many flippantly say because they changed after they got married. I hear it all the time: "Oh, I just outgrew my spouse." No they didn't!

People don't get divorced because they changed after they tie the knot. They divorce because they changed before they got married. Basically they went fishing and trolling. And during this dating and courtship "fishing time" together, they changed and sold out doing anything they could to "reel one another in like fish."

Once they landed the fish, neither one of them had to put on a show anymore nor finally did each become authentically real. Real means being shocked as the poor woman woke up after the first month, screaming, "I didn't know you burped every morning for fifty minutes and ate like a horse and hated to exercise! You faked me out at the gym; I thought we had that in common. You really don't think anything should be lifted if it doesn't have to be moved! I don't know the real you! Help!" And so they were no longer compatible and divorced.

ELIMINATING UNREALISTIC EXPECTATIONS

A 1990 Fortune Magazine article titled, “Why Grade A Executives Get An F As Parents,” detailed that children of successful executives are more likely to suffer a range of emotional and health-related problems than children of “less successful” parents. The article blamed it on the executives’ long hours and personal characteristics of impatience, perfectionism and efficiency and lack of tolerance for incompetence and irresponsibility.

What it didn’t say was how the executive’s organizations contributed to their problems as parents or what they might do to improve matters. How sad and typical that the author, like most of us, just blindly accepts the fact that work inevitably conflicts with family life, and that the organization is not responsible for balancing out work with family.

In my 35 years as a professional speaker I have seen an increase in concern over balancing family/work issues as one of the primary requests to be addressed in my talks. It’s always a tough assignment because in most cases the organization is broken, not just some of the individuals in it. The corporate culture simply expects, “If you want to get ahead around here, you must be willing to make sacrifices.”

Now I believe this when it comes to putting individual commitment demands on our selves and point it out throughout this book. But in an organizational scenario where these demands and pressures are placed on the individual from the top down, something has to give. Sacrifice is critical and often necessary, but only as long as the employees choose it.

Breakfast meetings, dinner meetings, travel, weekend retreats, and just plain long hours at the office because everyone is afraid to leave before the boss leaves and he/she doesn’t go home until seven, are all factors in this gross imbalance and negligence in dealing with family/work issues. The perception is that it’s best for the company. But how can it be if it’s not right for the employees? Many of these companies are the very organizations that have been singled out by authors as the standard bearers of what it means to be “Great.”

“WHAT DO YOU DO?”

I'm sorry, but if when asked what they do for a living, the employees describe the task they perform every day and not the purpose of the greater enterprise in which they take part, where is the sense of pride and loyalty and desire to increase productivity and profitability? When anyone sees them selves stuck in a system over which they have little influence, subconsciously they just "do their job," put in their minimum requirement time and try to cope with the forces outside of their control.

How sad! And to some degree, are we not all guilty? More often than we realize, the system causes the crisis, not external forces or competition, and yet we sit idly by and become victims of it.

It is my experience that the causes of both bad and good behavior – both high performance and minimum productivity – lie in a structure that either passively allows or blatantly encourages a certain type of thinking, expectation, and behavior. It does us no good to change ourselves if we don't change the organizations wherein we work and live, and visa-versa.

For these reasons, it is never enough to focus on what to know. We must focus on "what" to do, "why" we do, and "how" to do it. Rather than learning to get the job of our dreams, we must do whatever it takes to get the life of our dreams – the peace with freedom, the true happiness with purpose, and the results we desire, so we can live the life we deserve.

I read a survey of 100 Chief Financial Officers in the banking industry who responded to the same questions. Industry altering policy decisions were being made based on their answers. As I read them, I wondered what if the wrong people were in those key CFO positions. Their wrong personalities and wrong perceptions of success would taint and poison their answers, which in turn would change the way things were done industry-wide, and at the same time drastically affect whether they got what they wanted and wanted what they got.

I experienced this growing up, as my mother and father always told me I should be a lawyer. Throughout my childhood I constantly heard, "You'll make a heck of an attorney. You love to research, you're philosophical, seldom let go of your point of view, love to psychologically defend your causes and are argumentative when you believe you are in the right."

Thanks, but in retrospect, these same innate traits that could very well have made me an outstanding lawyer, might have given me a stroke and definitely would have made me a miserable person.

Just because I could have been the best attorney doesn't mean it was the right choice for me. We do this all the time in life, with ourselves, with our children, with our co-workers and partners. And because we can't get right answers from the wrong questions, we need to stop and think about the questions we are asking. "Is my son talented enough to play baseball?" is a very different question than, "Does my son want to play baseball?" A young woman considers the question, "Will you marry me?" when the question she needs to ask herself is, "Do I love him?"

It's absolutely true. In every industry and circumstance, in every relationship both personal and professional, the one who asks the questions is in complete control of the conversation. He or she who asks the right questions gets ahead faster and succeeds more frequently because they have the right answers that allow them to reach their expectations and accomplish their goals.

CHAPTER THIRTY-SIX

PARTNER LEADERSHIP IS MANAGEMENT PARTNER MANAGEMENT IS LEADERSHIP

Many suggest there is a huge difference between leadership and management. What do you think? The general perception is that management is old school and leadership is hip and now. From my experience in working with some of the most successful and unsuccessful companies in the world, I have seen firsthand that we have a major shortage of great managers in many of them. It is because of this leadership verses management mindset that keeps us believing they are completely different.

Leadership is certainly the "sexier" of the two, and some have abandoned developing excellent management skills because they want to be a leader, but management can be hip and now, and leadership can be old school. There are good leaders and poor leaders and there are good managers and poor managers.

For this reason I don't see managers and leaders as different people. The best and most successful business people, school administrators, and coaches all practice effective and contemporary management and will provide the leadership that their organizations require.

By definition, managers are responsible for taking care of business processes, planning, assignments, quality control, productivity, and the alignment of the organization. Management is the practice of tending to regular and emerging business needs. Great managers tend to the details of running the daily operation, problem solving, and if done efficiently, make it look easy.

Leaders are responsible for creating vision and identifying what needs to be done and why

Managers then take the 'What' and 'Why' and convert it into the 'How-To' and 'When.' Partner Leadership is about influencing, inspiring, encouraging, setting an amazing example through role-model -excellence, and communicating in a compelling way to employees, customers, and peers the purpose and direction of the organization. Partner Leaders have dreams for sale and passionately talk about the possibilities.

Managers decide upon goals based on necessity instead of desire and tend to be reactive since they focus on current information. Partner Leaders tend to be proactive since they envision and promote their ideas instead of reacting to current situations. Partner Leaders shape ideas instead of responding to them.

Most believe we are born with natural tendencies to either delight in the management details of dotting i's and crossing t's, or with a leadership ability to see the bigger picture with desire to lead. Some believe leadership cannot be taught, and if it is, according to the Harvard Business Review, learning must take place before the age of twenty-one.

But in my experience, especially through my many years watching and participating as a Character and Leadership Development Consultant with the United States Military – particularly at the Air Force Academy, at the Military Academy at West Point (Army) and as a regular lecturer at Air University, Maxwell Air Force Base, that both management and leadership attitudes and skills can and should be taught to everyone at all ages in every industry. Voila! The emergence of a Partner Leadership culture!

I have personally seen people from every demographic, socioeconomic condition, age, gender, race, and level of education learn to be leaders. Therefore, preparing differently to lead in every aspect and opportunity in our lives begins with the firm conviction that the military is famous for: To be a good leader you must be a good follower, and every day you will be required to both lead and follow. This means you are a leader some of the time and need to be a manager some of the time, but always constant and consistent in demonstrating your high level of both management and leadership prowess.

The good news is that the same things that influence you to be an extraordinary Partner Manager and Significant Partner Leader are the same things that influence others to want to join you: Beliefs, Attitude and Behavior, which determines how you communicate. The very best example of this is found in:

MASLOW'S HIERARCHY OF NEEDS

Maslow's Hierarchy of Needs is the most quoted theory in psychology that Abraham Maslow proposed in his 1943 paper A Theory of Human Motivation. His theory contends that as humans meet 'basic needs' they seek to satisfy successively 'higher needs' that occupy a set hierarchy.

Maslow's theory is often referred to as a pyramid consisting of five levels: the four lower levels are grouped together as Deficiency needs associated with physiological needs: Body Wellness, Comfort, Safety, Security, Love, Belonging, and Self Respect/Esteem. The top level is termed Growth needs, associated with psychological needs Maslow calls Self-Actualization.

While deficiency needs must be met, growth needs are continually shaping behavior. The basic concept is that the higher needs in this hierarchy only come into focus once all the needs that are lower down in the pyramid are mainly or entirely satisfied. Growth forces create upward movement in the hierarchy, whereas regressive forces push the peak performance needs further down.

Maslow's highest level is Self-Actualization which means: "the instinctual need of humans to make the most of their unique abilities and to strive to be the best they can be – the intrinsic growth of what is already in the organism." In other words, not to change, but to become more of who we already are!

With all due respect to Maslow, I have experienced a similar but different set of needs in my personal and professional lives, which resulted in the creation of my own Hierarchy of Needs illustrated in the forthcoming diagram. Because it is easier to identify a program than it is to implement a process, I offer five attributes that will assist us in the application of both Maslow's needs and the modified version I present. So far in my personal experience, I have found that everything anyone would ever want to be, begins and ends with being:

- Meek - "patient; enduring without resentment; teachable."
- Submissive - "surrendering to the authority or control of an-other; the condition of being humble; to yield oneself to the will of a higher power source."
- Loving - "having strong affection for another arising out of kinship and personal ties; affection based on admiration, benevolence, and common interests; unselfish devotion and loyal concern for the good of another."
- Charitable - "serving and doing something for a total stranger who can't do anything for you in return, knowing you won't get any credit."
- Disciplined – "He who requires much from himself and little from others, will keep himself from being the object of resentment. It is not the whip that makes men, but the lure of things that are worthy to be loved."
- Resolute – "Nothing can come of nothing. He that would have the fruit must climb the tree."
- Persistent – "Many strokes of the ax overthrow the tallest oaks. The racehorse is broken down in his speed, whilst the camel-driver jogs on with his beast to the end of his journey. Remember, a limping man is still walking."

Comprehending our true needs provides the motivation to endure to the end of the balancing process and to always do the right thing simply because it's the right thing to do, especially when no one is around. Your assignment is to familiarize yourself with this pyramid. Ponder how each of the five attributes makes possible the achievement of each need and how they drive you up the pyramid to satisfy the next higher need until you begin self-actualizing through self-expression.

HEIRACHY PYRAMID OF NEEDS

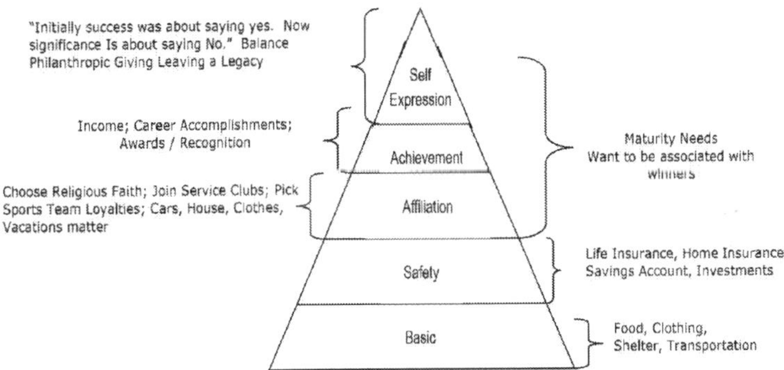

THE PATH OF A CHAMPION LEADER

Creating Self is a process that never ends as self-actualization and becoming successful is an everlasting work in progress. To help us sustain our motivation to continually stretch and improve, we need to surround ourselves with others of like mind and similar desired results. To help me, my dad told me at a young age to identify the thoroughbred champions of my generation and to keep in touch.

Consequently, I have some incredible famous friends who are successful and in influential positions in business, sports, the military, politics and high society. I knew them long before they became powerful, wealthy and well known, but looking back, not before they became successful.

At an early age they were doing the right things simply because they were the right things to do. They seemed to always stand out in the crowd and take the path less traveled because they always were stretching to satisfy their next highest need.

THOROUGHBRED CHAMPIONS

The thoroughbred champions of every generation walk on higher ground. That's what sets them apart. They relentlessly Create themselves into the persons they need to be by climbing the "pyramid of higher needs" that eventually makes them special, different, unique, faster, smarter, stronger. In fact, that's what makes them champions and puts them in the same category as the winner of a horse race.

For example, all horses competing in the Kentucky Derby are thoroughbred racing champions - as it is requisite for their entry into the race. But still only one emerges as the leader of leaders – the champion among champions.

In 1973, horse racing's Triple Crown Winner Secretariat set track records that still stand today. In the Kentucky Derby, Secretariat broke last but gradually moved up on the field in the backstretch, then over-took his rival Sham at the top of the stretch, pulling away to win the Derby by 2 1/2 lengths. On his way to a track record (1:59.25), he ran each quarter-mile segment faster than the one before it. This means he was still accelerating as of the final quarter-mile of the race when he crossed the finish line. No horse in history has ever run the Derby faster!

In the second leg of the Triple Crown, the Preakness Stakes, Secretariat broke last but then made a huge, last-to- first move on the first turn. After reaching the lead with 5 1/2 furlongs to go, Secretariat was never challenged and won by 2 1/2 lengths. The Maryland Jockey Club, which is responsible for maintaining Preakness records, recognizes 1:54.25 as the official time.

However, the Daily Racing Form for the first time in history, printed its own clocking of 1:53.25 next to the official time in the chart of the race making it a track record. As Secretariat prepared for the final competition of the Triple Crown, he appeared on the covers of three national magazines, Time Magazine, Newsweek, and Sports Illustrated. He had become a national celebrity.

In this third race, the Belmont Stakes, a crowd of 67,605, cheered as Secretariat set a fast early pace, opening ten lengths on the rest of the field. After the 6-furlong mark, Secretariat astonished spectators by continuing on the fast pace and opening up a larger and larger margin on the field. In the stretch, Secretariat opened a 1/16 mile lead on the other horses and at the finish, won by 31 lengths (breaking the mar-gin-of-victory record set by Triple Crown winner Count Fleet, who won by 25 lengths). Secretariat ran the fastest 1 1/2 miles on dirt in history, 2:24 flat, which broke the Stakes record by more than two seconds.

This works out to a speed of 37.5 mph for his entire performance and Secretariat's world record still stands. Secretariat became the first Triple Crown winner in twenty-five years and only the ninth champion in history. When Secretariat passed away the autopsy revealed that his heart was twice the size of an ordinary thoroughbred's heart! Hmmm.

YOU CAN . . . BUT WILL YOU BECOME A CHAMPION LEADER?

Obviously we can't know what Secretariat was thinking about when he worked out and took the track on race days, but we do know the reasons people in business, sports and the military become a champion's champion.

The bad news is that it's simple to learn to think and behave like champions do, which means there is no excuse for any of us to not follow them to higher ground. The good news is that it's only one or two steps up from where we are currently walking so it's within our immediate reach.

For example, in horse racing's 1978 competition for the Triple Crown, Affirmed emerged as the champion – only the eleventh Triple Crown champion in history, beating the same second place horse in all three races, just as Secretariat did. In the Kentucky Derby, Affirmed beat Alydar by 1 1/2 lengths. In the Preakness, Affirmed beat Alydar by only a neck. In the Belmont Stakes, Affirmed beat Alydar just by a nose!

The great news is that if some horses can dig deeper than their competitors, step it up when extra effort is necessary, and do whatever it takes to win even by a nose, so can we!

CHAPTER THIRTY-SEVEN

THE FORGOTTEN FUNDAMENTALS OF PARTNER LEADERSHIP

Let me share the interviews I had with five friends who just happen to be some of America's greatest corporate leaders. Ponder the following 14 questions and their answers, that you may experience the practical application of leadership The following five individuals held the listed job description, title, responsibility at the time of my interview:

Steve Munn, former CFO of Carrier Corporation and former president/CEO and chairman of the board of Carlisle Companies - Syracuse, New York.

Paul Raffin, president of Express Limited (retail clothier conglomerate/ Victoria Secret - Columbus, Ohio).

Rick Larsen, former president and CEO of Operation "OK" Kids Charities (an international not-for-profit corporation – Current Director of the Sutherland Institute - Salt Lake City, Utah).

Nikki Waters, senior vice president of strategic business development/prepaid commercial services division of First Data Corporation (San Diego, California).

Barry Raber, founder, president/CEO of Business Property Trust (real estate investment & management firm - Portland, Oregon).

KEY QUESTIONS AND CRUCIAL ANSWERS FROM CORPORATE LEADERS

1. You are a very successful and respected leader. In your experience and opinion, what is the single most important quality or trait necessary to succeed?

Steve Munn: There is no one single most important quality or trait necessary to succeed. One cannot run a company, or one's life, by sound bites, words, or slogans. Leadership requires a skill set of qualities and traits. Everything and everybody is constantly changing or bringing new items to evaluate. One needs a number of skills and assets to respond. A committed leader will want to always improve, and this will require a set of skills and traits to positively influence people, markets, products, and strategy.

Raffin: Listening in order to learn and discover.

Larsen: It is a necessary combination of passion and tenacity.

Waters: Passion. A leader who is passionate about the achievement of his or her vision and goal, while constantly keeping the customer's best interests in sight, along with those of the company, its employees, and the needs of the ultimate end user, creates an environment where all parties involved work together to realize the achievement.

Raber: Desire. Some call it "fire in the belly." For me it comes from something that happened to me that made me feel I had something to prove.

2. What is your greatest quality or trait?

Munn: Perhaps the ability to care about what needs to be accomplished. In other words, the ability to execute and simultaneously focus on achieving that mission or objective.

Raffin: Translator, synthesizer.

Larsen: I really refuse to quit. I will come at things a hundred different ways, but I just can't quit if I believe in it.

Waters: A relentless thirst for knowledge, and then applying that which is gained to new ideas, improving processes and sharing with others for greater understanding.

Raber: Possibility thinking. I think anything is possible and, therefore, I am the master of my own destiny. This makes for a wonderful life.

3. What is the single most important secret to your personal success?

Munn: There is no single secret to my personal success.

Raffin: The ability to articulate a point of view.

Larsen: This may sound odd, but I don't really believe I am the only guy who could do this. I feel I have unique gifts that make me suited, but that alone is not enough. I feel I need to work harder than anyone else, and that I am truly lucky to be where I am. I am not sure what a shrink would do with that, but it makes every day a blessing as well as a challenge and opportunity.

Waters: Realizing success from seeing those who have worked for me succeed.

Raber: Optimism.

4. Do you believe a corporate culture should be a mirror image of the CEO's personality and what matters most to the CEO? Why?

Munn: No. A CEO's personality plays a role, but there are many, many influences on a company's culture.

Raffin: No. Corporate culture is an entity based upon the values that all employees cherish and practice. The CEO is simply a visible example of those values at work. His or her most important role is to "live" these values and reward those who do the same.

Larsen: Yes, but the CEO has some serious responsibility. There must be some level of mirroring. Not to the extent of a dictatorial "do it my way" culture; that would stifle creativity. But the company needs to mirror the passion and commitment of the CEO. I think sometimes that is where companies become confused. If you take every aspect of a CEO, you will get what else? An imperfect human being. If a staff becomes focused on the imperfections, or if those imperfections become a liability, the staff may become hesitant to mirror any-thing else in the CEO. This puts a significant amount of pressure on a CEO to be the "right guy." He must find a way to get past his own personality and convey vision. Vision and passion from the top can be exciting, or they can be a mess. If a CEO is always running a step ahead of the staff or fighting the culture, something has to give. Again, if the CEO is sure of where he is going, I feel he must build a staff that "buys in" or will mirror the key aspects of their leader, at least in terms of commitment and passion.

Waters: There are many different manners for a corporate culture to evolve (particularly with the continual mergers and acquisitions of organizations), notwithstanding the personality of the CEO. I believe that the corporate culture does reflect the personality of the CEO, yet in turn, those in a decision-making role must also ensure that the culture allows for accomplishment of the goal in a manner that fosters integrity, long-term success, and relationship building with a broad base of constituents. In a public company, a CEO will always want to accomplish the targeted earnings for shareholders, with those that are successful doing so in a way that attracts and retains talent as well as customers.

Raber: It can, but in order to last 20 to 30 to 100 years, it should not. In order to last, the culture has to be a set of processes, policies, creeds, visions, and mission statements that bridge many CEOs. If the CEO's personality served the business, then those things should be woven into the culture and perpetuated, as in the cases of Southwest Airlines and Disney, which have done this with their founders.

5. What's the most important quality you look for when hiring a new employee?

Munn: New employees must bring a skill set of attributes to a company; some will be strong, others won't be as strong. But a set of qualities is needed, not just one most important.

Raffin: Honesty - to keep their promises

Larsen: Passion. You can always teach skills, but you can't force people to care enough to sacrifice.

Waters: I look for enthusiasm, confidence in their abilities, yet humility to recognize the need to continue to learn and grow professionally. Honesty (although sometimes difficult to con-firm in an interview process) is critical as well as independent thinking.

Raber: A can-do-attitude.

6. Do you hire more for knowledge, skill, or for attitude? Rank in order.

Munn: Depends upon the position, the company's needs, and the circumstances surrounding the hire. I've hired for all three; and all three have probably been ranked 1, 2, or 3 at some point in time.

Raffin: First, attitude; second, skill; and third, knowledge. Attitude cannot be taught. Skill allows the new employee to hit the ground running and garner respect from fellow employees and leaders. Knowledge can be provided. In this context there is no difference between a best and a right employee. Attitude, skill, and knowledge are mutually dependent traits. I person-ally do not believe in classifying right vs. wrong because all employees have the opportunity to make a contribution.

Larsen: Attitude, skill, and then knowledge. Again, you can always learn the fine points - expand your knowledge. But knowledge alone in no way automatically translates into action and passion. Otherwise, no one would smoke or be overweight or be disloyal to a spouse or family. Everyone knows these things are not a good idea, and yet every day millions of people do them anyway.

Waters: This truly depends on the position. In general, I would rank these attributes in the following order: Attitude first, skill, and then knowledge.

Raber: Attitude first, no doubt. Then they have to be bright. In order to really help the company, the employees need to be smart and savvy enough to know the "why" behind things. That way they can help change the company for the better. Job knowledge would be second and skill last. The best person at the job may not be best for the company or team. The right employee fits the culture, gets along well with others, adds to the success equation, and is just good at what they do. Disney calls it the "right fit talent."

7. What is loyalty? Do you "buy" it or create it? How?

Munn: It would be hard for me to believe one can buy loyalty. Loyalty evolves over time, resulting from predictability, support in both good and bad times, accompanying responsibility with authority, and allowing and supporting independent and outside-the-box thinking.

Raffin: Loyalty is what a person thinks in their quietest, most private moments - how they feel about the company they work for, no compromises, and no sense that they must be-come some other version of themselves when they enter the work environment.

Larsen: You can buy it from some people, but only temporarily. As soon as they get offered more, they shift loyalties. Loyalty, in my opinion, must first exist for the cause or the purpose and can then expand into personal loyalty to others who share your passion.

Waters: Loyalty is a person's desire to support (which can take on many different forms) an organization, industry, employee, or cause. I do not believe it can be bought but that it is created from those who share the same vision and have a like desire to attain the same goal. It also comes from creating a culture of trust and caring for individuals - helping them be successful and acknowledging their contributions.

Raber: You can't buy it. Money can influence it, but real, true, authentic loyalty is created. Loyalty is the brother to trust. Each takes time to learn and develop, and all are based mostly on human relationships.

8. Do you believe you should develop and promote leadership and management from within? Why or why not?

Munn: Leadership should be developed from within. Why? Because it's cheaper to do so, strategies are better understood and implemented, market reactions are quicker, mistakes are recognized earlier, and commitment and loyalty are developed as the employer sees their own - as well as themselves - moving to more responsible positions.

Raffin: Yes. Leadership is an organic and holistic characteristic of companies that care about their people, their products, and the effect those products have in the world and the community. If a company is consciously competent in creating and living by a set of values that embrace and sustain a collaborative caring culture, then great leaders will emerge from it. This is a great way of preserving and evolving the DNA of the corporate entity.

Larsen: Case by case. I have not ever discerned a clear pattern. It seems situational to me. I will say this: If there is an expectation of leadership promotion, or if the norm is advancement from within, it seems to create an atmosphere of entitlement. On the other hand, if there is no chance, why put in the time? People need to know that performance, not time spent, equals advancement. Clearly the opportunity must be there. However, the criteria must be well-thought-out enough so that all parties can see how decisions are ultimately made.

Waters: I do believe in the development and promotion of leadership and management from within as long as the right talent exists inside the organization. Yet, I also have hired out-side talent to bring a broader dimension to the knowledge base as well as introduce fresh ideas from one who has gained experience from other organizations.

Raber: Within for sure. I have never seen it work from hiring from outside. No one will respect anyone who did not come up through the ranks. An outsider cannot possibly understand the nuances of the culture. Now if the company is completely broken and going broke, an outsider may succeed, but in a healthy company I would say almost never.

9. What makes your business model successful while so many others fail?

Munn: I really don't want to get into that question.

Raffin: A founder who remembers what it is like to serve one customer at a time and has made great efforts at preserving that entrepreneurial spirit in the face of a large, complex organization.

Larsen: What we are doing here has never been done before. While we are experiencing great early success, I think we have yet to prove that we are a long-term success. That is our toughest challenge; we cannot stop where we are and consider our-selves a success. For all we have done to this point, there is so much more to do. However, there is a branding strategy underlying a pure passion for children's causes that if we do prove "staying power," that branding and focus will be the differentiator.

Waters: I have worked for good leaders, very poor leaders, and an exceptional leader. I remember how I felt working for each person and what I accomplished. All of these experiences have helped me to try to emulate that which I learned from the exceptional leader, while avoiding the shortcomings of the very poor leaders.

Raber: A great Hedgehog (see Good to Great, by Jim Collins).

10. Have you ever made a drastic change in your company's direction, philosophy, or mission? If so, what was it? What motivated you? Was it successful? If not, what would you do differently?

Munn: Yes. We significantly changed the strategic direction from computer-associated products to a return to the core business. We additionally changed the culture from a re-turn-on-assets-driven incentive program to a growth-with-returns culture. The motivation was driven from observing the company's stock, which had gone essentially nowhere for seven to eight years. We needed to get competitive and grow the core strength, or the entire company would be in trouble. It was successful.

Raffin: We attempted two drastic pieces of re-engineering in the past three years - a right-sizing initiative that resulted in a nearly 40 percent reduction in expenses and a major repositioning effort aimed at trading up to a more luxury-based product line aimed at an older clientele. Neither of these initiatives was successful and left the company in a severe crisis mode from which we are just beginning to recover. The vision that led to both ideas should have been passionately debated and discussed prior to launching. However, given the hierarchical culture and decision-making process that is in place, this did not present a possibility at the time.

Larsen: Not drastic but painful. As we have grown, the need for absolute focus has caused management and philosophy changes. While I would not call them drastic, they were certainly significant, and all stemmed from a pure passion for what we do. It has been successful to date and, in fact, sent a message, inside and out, that this is going to be a different kind of company. The only thing I would have done differently was move sooner, given the chance.

Waters: I have never been shy about being a change agent, and if I am passionate about the value of implementing change. I will be tenacious toward moving the needle. I have spent the better part of the past eighteen months introducing a very processing-oriented company to the benefits and value of migrating to a more marketing-focused company that truly values the needs of the customer and drives toward excellence. The motivation was recognizing the value that this approach could bring in earnings per share, customer relationships, and the long -term benefits within the industry. It was successful to small degrees, where seeds were planted that have begun to take root.

Raber: Never made a drastic move. Have not had to, but would if survival and success required it.

11. Would you hire someone who wants your job and is qualified for it?

Munn: Yes, absolutely. At any level, this is a very desirable trait.

Raffin: Absolutely. I would love to hire any individual who possesses the drive and desire to run an organization such as ours while embracing the values we believe in - those who do not, by nature, promote individual success over team success.

Larsen: Yes. I am not going to live forever, but I would like to see what we have started here live at least that long!

Waters: Yes, knowing that it is imperative to have depth within an organization and be planning for succession.

Raber: Depends on the life stage of the company. At the early stages of a company, no. But at a mature stage like I am in today, then yes, of course.

12. Would you hire you?

Munn: Yes.

Raffin: Yes, I would.

Larsen: In a minute. And the reason is this: I know I will figure out a way to get the job done. No one would ever have to ask or even suggest that I come in early, stay late, or try one more time. I just would.

Waters: I would, and I would even challenge myself!

Raber: Yes.

13. Would you want you for a boss? Why or why not?

Munn: Yes, because I would be given responsibility and authority and would be supported in exploring all menus toward success.

Raffin: I would. I encourage a pursuit of discovery and learning together within a spirit of collaboration and mutual respect. I work very hard at fostering this, including teaching executives how to maintain an open mind and heart and to vocalize their ideas in ways that are not exclusionary. I believe people are, by nature, open organisms that respond best when they feel the freedom to pursue their dreams and share their aspirations.

Larsen: If I loved the job and the mission, yes. If I were just looking for a job, any job, I would be a horrible guy to work for.

Waters: In most cases, yes, since I believe the experience and drive for excellence would benefit me. If I did not have the same level of interest to initiate and the ability to question the norm and seek out information, then I would be difficult to work with.

Raber: At first I thought "no" because I was too much of a hard ass. Now I think I would. I have extremely high expectations of my team, and I like supervisors who have had high of me.

14. When it's all over, how do you want to be remembered personally? Professionally?

Munn: It is not important how I am remembered. It is meaningful how I act while still here because today's actions may make a positive contribution. Memories are fine, but they wear and are misunderstood with time.

Raffin: Both in the same way - as one who emptied himself in order to be filled by the wisdom of others and who, in turn, provided a loving, caring center of support.

Larsen: I gave it all I had, and I made a difference. That's really all anyone could want.

Waters: Personally, as a generous person of positive spirit and giving to others. Professionally, as a wonderful mentor who will always be remembered by those with whom I worked as a person they wanted to emulate.

Raber: I would like to be loved. Hopefully someone will love me as husband and father, and others will love me as a friend, business partner, boss, and fun-loving mentor. There are so many different relationships out there. I hope to be loved by all who really knew me!

CHAPTER THIRTY-EIGHT

A SIGNIFICANT PARTNER LEADER'S RESPONSIBILITY IS TO MENTOR

"I'd rather see a sermon preached than hear one any day
- I'd rather you would walk with me than merely point the way"

When it comes to being a Significant Partner Leader, persuading through influence, or mentoring, I always think of educators of any kind and honor them with my published statement, "Teaching is the profession that makes all other professions possible. No one in our world would have a job if it weren't for a teacher. Teachers are the smartest people on the planet and could work for any corporation or elite organization, and yet they give up money and privilege to teach us what we need to know to make our dreams come true.

Because of its critical importance to every individual who ever became significant, let's wind down this Leadership Manual with laser-like focus on the single most important job description of a leader - the one commitment that takes you from successful to significance. It's similar to, but the highbred version of teaching and coaching, affectionately called Mentoring.

Mentoring is a shared experience that proves when the water in the lake goes up, all the boats rise together. I learned this when my uncle took a bunch of us roller-skating for the first time and I looked like a newborn deer with my legs flopping everywhere. My uncle was an amazing skater and came up behind me and whispered, "Take my hands in a cross grip and watch my feet."

As he helped me balance while he skated by my side, I was able to see and feel the rhythm of his back and forth sliding motion. Within minutes, I could mimic what he was doing with his arms and feet. When I could do it on my own, he let go and I had the time of my life!

THE CURRENCY OF MENTORING IS IDEAS

Just as we began this book by pointing out the Napoleon Hill observation that "Thoughts are things," I conclude this book with the same emphasis, but in a Mentorship role.

There is no such thing as a financial crisis, only an idea crisis. Ideas create income, and when it comes to mentoring, everything begins as an idea. The currency of mentoring is ideas. Mentors don't tell and give answers, they only teach how to craft the right, better questions and stir curiosity within those whom they are mentoring, that they may also be able to ask better questions to get the better answers when their mentor is not there to help.

If music is the international currency of peace, and a smile is the international currency of friendship, then ideas are the international currency of success and happiness. A mentor knows and teaches that true innovation requires wonder. Wondering who you are, where you came from, why you're here on earth, and where you're going when you die – is requisite to reaching your full potential, which creates success and happiness.

A Mentor knows and teaches that innovation, wonderment, and curiosity are not sometime things, they are all the time mental states fueled by passion, creativity, and imagination; that it's not enough to have a good idea once in a while.

We must constantly think and re-think and come up with great ideas, and then let them marinate and percolate into better questions, which lead to much better ideas. Spontaneous innovation and/or invention is a myth, as better ideas can only turn into best and right solutions, products and services through an incubation period of reflection, patience and a continuation of passion, creativity, imagination and wonderment. When it comes to mentoring, three things are clear:

- "Give a man a fish and you feed him for a day. Teach a man to fish and he feeds himself for a lifetime." There must be a constant flow and continuous exchange of ideas between mentor and mentee.
- Albert Einstein said that what distinguished him from others was his ability to ask childlike questions. Remember, Albert was no "Einstein" when he was in school. He became "one" as he perfected the art of questioning.
- The word inspire means to "breathe life into," and a Mentor breathes reality and clarity into the mind and heart of who he is mentoring. Just as amazing authors such as Ernest Hemingway mentored through his words that "whether facing a charging beast or in the heat of battle, it brought about a moment of clarity from which you could write a clearer and truer picture by immersing yourself in that moment whatever it turned out to be."

Bottom line: Extraordinary Mentors are inspirational by nature and do all they know how to do to make sure there are extraordinary inspirational leaders.

INSPIRATIONAL QUALIFICATIONS

There is a huge difference between inspiration and motivation. Significant Partner Leaders know that Inspiration affects attitude—the way we think and the lens through which we see life. Motivation affects behavior—the way we act.

Therefore, no one can really motivate another. Partner Leaders know that the only thing we can ever hope to do is paint a bigger, brighter picture to inspire one another to want to motivate ourselves. Most of the time, peak performance—taking ourselves to the next level, stretching and becoming everything we were born to be—is inspired from without until we see it, want it, buy into it, and own it to the degree that it comes from within.

It has been said, "There are no heroes—only ordinary men and women caught in extraordinary circumstance who place service before self." It has also been said that you can't lead where you won't go, and you can't teach what you don't know. I agree, and therefore I don't necessarily respect and follow someone just because he practices what he preaches.

Inspiring people preach only what they practice. Inspiration implies that you know something and do something with what you know. To be an effective manager requires character. To be an effective leader requires credibility. To be inspirational in another person's life requires both character and credibility. Hence, Significant Partner Leadership is Management and Significant Partner Management is Leadership.

It's motivating to see a person beat the odds when placed in a situation that requires great fortitude and action. It's inspiring to read about a prisoner of war who survives to write about how he handled torture and made it through his ordeal. I know a handful of heroes. Two are real heroes who, through their character and credibility, inspire all who know them. They are Hal Hornburg, a retired US Air Force Four Star General, and my dear father, S. Wayne Clark.

INSPIRING HEROES

Webster's Dictionary defines a hero as "a mythological or legendary figure often of divine descent endowed with great strength or ability; an illustrious warrior; a man or woman admired for achievements and noble qualities; one that shows superior courage; the central figure in an event, period, or movement who is the object of extreme devotion; someone's idol; a role model leading by example, inspiring with character, facing all fear, self-sacrificing and exhibiting or marked by daring."

General Hornburg (ret. U.S. Air Force) is a great American, former command fighter pilot, influential world leader, multiple war hero, devoted husband, father, grandfather, musician, athlete, and a trusted friend of mine. He mentors people through his deeds and his words:

- "People first, mission always."
- "Leadership at the lowest level is about presence, programs, and people. Leadership at the highest level is about passion, principles, and people."
- "We rise higher and see further standing not only on the strong shoulders of those who have gone before us, but also on the shoulders of those who are currently under our command, supporting us and following our lead."
- "A celebrity is a big name - a hero is a big man."
- "Quality of life is more than new furniture."
- "You recruit the individual, but you must retain the family."
- "We enter the armed forces to serve our country, but we fight for our teammates, for each other, for our 'band of brothers' battle buddies fighting beside us."

General Hornburg knows and reminds us that transformation is an inside-out job—that you really can take an eighteen year-old who barely graduated from high school and has been a cocky, undisciplined Attention Deficit Disorder-labeled student, put him through a six-week Basic Cadet Training boot camp course at Lackland Air Force Base in San Antonio, Texas, and turn him into a respectful, disciplined, patriotic young man.

All the Air Force did was give him purpose, high expectations, responsibility, self-respect, extraordinary trust, and an opportunity to be a part of something larger and more important than himself. Then, through training and a couple years of experience, he is put in charge of a $50 million jet—maintaining it, or fixing it, or keeping it combat-ready, or flying it. General Hornburg knows that what the Air Force does with 37,000 recruits each year is unveil to them what is already inside of them.

"You can if you think you can," is more of a powerful transformational mantra than anyone can imagine. General Hornburg leaves an inspirational legacy that will always be remembered: "In any endeavor, people matter most—we are in the people-building business!"

INSPIRATIONAL DAD

My dad, S. Wayne Clark, clearly my superhero, taught me in word and in deed: "Any Male Can Be A Father – But It Takes A Special Man To Be A Dad!"

Dad was a legislator, pilot, US Air Force officer, cotton farmer, silver miner, rancher, entrepreneur who started his own insurance company, owner of two large cemeteries/mortuaries, and creator of a successful financial corporation. He still made time for church and family, and he always did, and still does, inspire me with his actions and wisdom:

- "When everybody thinks alike, nobody thinks very much."
- "Growth is good, but growth without good growth is no growth."
- "Giving half effort doesn't get you half results - it gets you no results."
- "Unless you try something beyond what you have mastered, you will never grow."
- "It's not how much you make, but how much you spend - nickels make dollars."
- "We get what we inspect, not what we expect."
- "Knowledge is awareness of the fact that fire will burn wisdom is remembrance."
- "Remember who you are; any male can be a father, but it takes a special man to be a dad."

- “Significance and peace of mind can only come through living on purpose with someone to love, something to do, and someplace to go, in order to feel wanted, important, loved, and capable.”
- “Clear conscience with pure joy comes only when we choose to fill our minds with truth, fill our hearts with love, and fill our lives with service.”
- “What you are today is the result of what you have thought up to this moment. What you will be tomorrow depends upon the thoughts you think from now on.”

LAST LECTURE

Let’s conclude this book with the ultimate Significant Partner Leadership legacy question: If you only had one day to live and this was your Last Lecture, what would your Significant Partner Leadership mentoring message be? I definitely would include:

- Be you - you’ll make a lousy somebody else.
- Every government could be better – vote.
- The greatest novel has not yet been written - write it.
- The most inspirational music is yet to come - listen.
- Only 2 percent of all knowledge is known - imagine and study.
- The greatest sports records have yet to be broken - dream and work.
- The regrets you’ll have when you die are not regarding the things you did, but the things you wish you had done - leave no regrets.
- • Significance is knowing not every day is a good day, but you live anyway; not everyone will tell you the truth, but you are honest anyway; not all deals are fair, but you play fair anyway; not everyone you love will love you back, but you love anyway; and although you are scared to death, you saddle up anyway.

I would then conclude this Last Lecture by stating that God put me on earth to accomplish a certain number of things, but because I am so far behind, I will never die!

For A One Hour Keynote Speech,
A One Day Leadership School,
or A Full Three Day Personal and Professional Development Training on Implementing The Life Changing Content In Dan's Best Selling Book:

The Art of Significance

- Achieving The Level Beyond Success

PLEASE CONTACT:

WEBSITE: danclark.com
EMAIL: dan@danclark.com
OFFICE: 800-676-1121

THE ART OF SIGNIFICANT LEADERSHIP EDUCATION AND PERSONAL DEVELOPMENT COURSE™

An Interactive Experiential Experience For Emerging Leaders, Seasoned Corporate Executives, Entrepreneurs, Military Officers/NCOs, Government Civil Servants, And Educators Who Want To Transform Themselves And Their Organizations From Successful To Significance. The most comprehensive Leadership Education/Personal Development Course offered anywhere in the world! Flexible Schedules – Customized Content To Deal With Specific Issues And Needs

To provide specialized advanced instruction on Relationship Management, Conflict Resolution, and Empowering Yourself to the Highest Levels of Leadership. It is our experience that every participant will graduate with the necessary beliefs and skills required to assume the highest achieve every Level Beyond Success!

OTHER AVAILABLE BOOKS BY DAN CLARK

The Art of Significance -Achieving The Level Beyond Success
(Audiobook Also Available)

The Art of Significant Relationships
– An Anthology of 15 Experts On What, Why and How

The Art of Raising Significant Children

The Art of Significant Leadership
– How to Grow People Into Passionate Partners

The Art of Significant Selling
– How To Get People To Choose You Instead Of Just Somebody Who Does What You Do

The Art of Significant Team Building
– Where Self-Mastery is Permanent, Winning is Personal and High Performance is Automatic

The Art of Significant Speaking and Storytelling
– What I Learned From Zig Ziglar That You Should Know

The Art of Significant Network Marketing
(Audiobook and Study Guide)

Chicken Soup for the College Soul

The Most Popular Stories By Dan Clark In
Chicken Soup For The Soul

Puppies for Sale
(Illustrated Children's Hard Cover Storybook)

Clark's Children's Classics

Soul Food
- The Complete Dan Clark Story Collection

Puppies for Sale and Other Inspirational Tales

Dan Clark's Humor File
– A Repository of Jokes and B.S. Tales

The Treasury of Dan Clark Quotes, Lyrics and Poems